Leadership
and Futuring

The Practicing Administrator's Leadership Series
Jerry J. Herman and Janice L. Herman, Editors

ROADMAPS
TO SUCCESS

Other Titles in This Series Include:

The Path to School Leadership: A Portable Mentor
Lee G. Bolman and Terrence E. Deal

Holistic Quality: Managing, Restructuring, and Empowering Schools
Jerry J. Herman

Selecting, Managing, and Marketing Technologies
Jamieson A. McKenzie

Individuals With Disabilities: Implementing the Newest Laws
Patricia F. First and Joan L. Curcio

Violence in the Schools: How to Proactively Prevent and Defuse It
Joan L. Curcio and Patricia F. First

Women in Administration: Facilitators for Change
L. Nan Restine

Power Learning in the Classroom
Jamieson A. McKenzie

Computers: Literacy and Learning
A Primer for Administrators
George E. Marsh II

Restructuring Schools: Doing It Right
Mike M. Milstein

Reporting Child Abuse:
A Guide to Mandatory Requirements for School Personnel
Karen L. Michaelis

Handbook on Gangs in Schools:
Strategies to Reduce Gang-Related Activities
Shirley R. Lal, Dhyan Lal, and Charles M. Achilles

Conflict Resolution: Building Bridges
Neil H. Katz and John W. Lawyer

Resolving Conflict Successfully: Needed Knowledge and Skills
Neil H. Katz and John W. Lawyer

Preventing and Managing Conflict in Schools
Neil H. Katz and John W. Lawyer

Secrets of Highly Effective Meetings
Maria M. Shelton and Laurie K. Bauer

(see back cover for additional titles)

Leadership and Futuring

Making Visions Happen

John R. Hoyle

CORWIN PRESS, INC.
A Sage Publications Company
Thousand Oaks, California

For information address:

Corwin Press, Inc.
A Sage Publications Company
2455 Teller Road
Thousand Oaks, California 91320

SAGE Publications Ltd.
6 Bonhill Street
London EC2A 4PU
United Kingdom

SAGE Publications India Pvt. Ltd.
M-32 Market
Greater Kailash I
New Delhi 110 048 India

Printed in the United States of America

Library of Congress Cataloging-in-Publication Data

Hoyle, John.
    Leadership and futuring: making visions happen. / John R. Hoyle.
        p.   cm. — (Roadmaps to success)
    Includes bibliographical references.
    ISBN 0-8039-6300-9 (pbk.)
    1. Leadership. 2. Planning.   I. Title.   II. Series.
HD57.7.H69   1995
658.4'092—dc20   95-14648

This book is printed on acid-free paper.

95 96 97 98 99 10 9 8 7 6 5 4 3 2 1

Corwin Press Production Editor: S. Marlene Head

Contents

CORWIN
PRESS

The Corwin Press logo—a raven striding across an open book—
represents the happy union of courage and learning. We are a
professional-level publisher of books and journals for K-12 educators, and we are committed to creating and providing resources
that embody these qualities. Corwin's motto is "Success for All
Learners."

Foreword

John R. Hoyle, in this easily read, short volume titled *Leadership and Futuring: Making Visions Happen*, combines four important elements. He discusses (a) leaders who have influenced him, (b) a variety of other leaders he wishes he had known, (c) strategic planning for visions of *what should be* in the future, and (d) practical exercises for the reader who wishes to become a visionary leader.

He brings his messages to the reader in an entertaining manner, using such examples and techniques as a Leadership Comparison Checklist; the "Goodyear Blimp Vision"; and Scenario Writing, including a scenario for the year 2015.

In addition, a series of references and an annotated bibliography of the primary resources on this topic are provided for those who wish to explore further.

This well-known and creative author has produced a delightful and practical little guidebook. We recommend it highly for broadening everyone's leadership horizons.

Jerry J. Herman
Janice L. Herman
Series Co-Editors

Acknowledgments

I wish to thank my students and colleagues for the many ideas that they have shared with me and that are on each page of this book. I owe much to Texas A&M University for the freedom I have to teach, conduct research, and consult, and I thank Boston University for allowing me to teach in Europe in 1985-1986. These opportunities expanded my thinking on the use of futuring and visioning to prepare better leaders and organizations. I am indebted to the College of Agriculture at Texas A&M University for the opportunity to participate in Project 2020 Vision Workshops to sharpen my visioning saw under the expert guidance of Peter Bishop of the University of Houston Clear Lake. I thank my friend and coworker Bill Ashworth, whose word processing skills and patience were critical to the final product. As always, I am deeply grateful to my scholar spouse Carolyn Hoyle, who read and edited each page and makes life a true gift. Finally, I dedicate the book to the three heroes found in Chapter 1.

About the Author

John R. Hoyle specializes in leadership development and future studies. He has written or edited several books and has produced 90 articles and book chapters on organizational and leadership issues. One of his books, coauthored with Fenwick English and Betty Steffy, titled *Skills for Successful School Leaders* (1985), is in its second edition and was revised in 1994. It is one of the most widely used textbooks in the field of educational administration. Dr. Hoyle has served as President of the National Council of Professors of Educational Administration, the AASA Professor of the Year, and chaired the AASA National Commission on Standards for the Superintendency in 1993. He has been labeled an educational futurist in interviews by *U.S. News and World Report, Omni Magazine,* and *USA Today.* Dr. Hoyle is Professor of Educational Administration at Texas A&M University, where he teaches classes in future studies, organizational theory, and program evaluation, and holds a university award for distinguished achievement in teaching. A popular keynote speaker and workshop consultant, he works with schools, universities, agricultural agencies, and businesses in the United States and abroad. A student athlete at Texas A&M University, he spent several years as a teacher, coach, and administrator in the public schools and has taught in five universities and in Europe. Dr. Hoyle holds a Ph.D. in education and social science from Texas A&M University.

Introduction

Come on now, admit it, wouldn't you like to be viewed by others as a visionary leader with the charisma to make things happen? Reading this book and applying the suggested skills for personal and team improvement may not suddenly make you a charismatic visionary, but perhaps you can add another layer to your leadership ability.

This book is about broadening your skills to create new and exciting learning organizations and, in the words of Henry Kissinger, "Take people where they are and take them to places they have never been." Visionaries and their visions have inspired the creation of magnificent monuments that have withstood the ravages of time. The Greek temples, the Roman Coliseum, the chateaus of France, and Epcot Center had their genesis in someone's vision. According to Warren Bennis and Burt Namus, vision promotes a condition that is significantly better than the status quo by expressing a realistic, credible, and attractive organizational future. They speak metaphorically of vision as a target that beckons. Visions of shared leadership and bottom-up empowered organizations based on relationships are the new rage in organizational design. The traditional, top-down, bureaucratic, controlling model has gone the way of the typewriter. Well-oiled, predictable, clockwork systems are turning into less precise, team-based learning organizations that are creative, unpredictable, and "messy," and make up things as they go along. This transformation causes discomfort for managers who have a need to control and stay on top of all personnel and their job responsibilities. Other administrators have developed greater tolerance for ambiguity; have high boiling points; and thrive on information from research, reading, and constant interaction with others about new ideas. This new leader is a creative gadabout who helps design corporate futures through visioning and persuading others to share the vision. These new leaders in new organizations must be better prepared in the art and science of administration and futuring than those of the past. Future leaders must be exciting personalities who have a passion for what they do and can share the passion in a vision to capture the imagination and energy of others. The old saying, "You can't light a fire with a wet match," means more than ever to an aspiring leader in education and other human service organizations. "Empowerment," "site-based decision making," and "shared visions" are the catchwords of the day, but unless there is an energetic, talented visionary to light the fire of others, very few visions will be realized. Visionary leaders seem to create team loyalty, ideas, goals, and shared values. William F. May, an authority on leadership, believes that leaders must create goals, and that means going into the "x" of the future.

The best and most proven way to learn the skills of visionary leadership is to observe or read about those we admire. Chapter 1 is about six visionary leaders who embodied visionary leadership. Three of these leaders are my heroes, who shaped my life and career. The other three were visionaries of history who, by their acts of courage, caring, communication, and persistence, inspired millions of others to find the best in themselves and to share their visions for a better world. Each of the six visionaries had his or her own leadership style and personality, but three key characteristics stand out to serve as guideposts for this book. A capacity for caring for others is the first and most important characteristic of their vision. Second, each leader had a clear message that was communicated in simple, persuasive words; the third characteristic was the commitment to persist under the most difficult of circumstances. These three attributes must be present if a vision is to become a reality to make organizations more effective, inclusive, and supportive places. The review of the lives and contributions of these leaders offer the readers a chance to reflect on their own personal role models who have helped shape their leadership styles and careers and to gain insights into the attractive ingredients of visionary leadership.

Chapter 2 gives an overview of futurism as a field of study and presents the use of futuring to create shared visions that stress the "end in mind." The futuring process is based on motivating others. Because personal visions are the most motivating, the role of the visionary leader is to persuade others to rally around a "cause beyond themselves" that will increase their personal visions into shared visions for the organization.

Chapter 3 includes strategies and inspirational stories about successful visionaries who transformed visions into realities and overcame the problems they faced. The importance of proper timing, good data, and financial support are presented to assist the leader in realizing the vision. The chapter ends with an account of a visionary environmentalist and his futuristic community of Matfield Green in Kansas.

Chapter 4 contains a variety of step-by-step futuring techniques to enliven workshops for learning skills to create real-world programs. Five group and individual futuring activities are included, with special emphasis on scenario development.

Chapter 5 offers practical challenges and suggestions to help the reader become a better visionary leader who can make things happen by focusing on developing a greater capacity for caring, improving communication through persuasion and listening, and strengthening the resolve to persist and to finish the races worth finishing. I hope that the reader will gain greater knowledge and inspiration from this work and "become better than you think you can be." Oliver Wendell Holmes believed that the potency within us far outweighs the accomplishments of the past or the challenges of the present and future.

Leaders I Have Known and Others I Wish I Had Known

To write about visionary leaders is a little difficult if you have never seen one. I am fortunate because I have seen several and have been inspired by them. Historians record the lives of extraordinary visionaries who inspired people during their lives and made lasting contributions. This chapter includes the lives and influence of three visionary leaders I knew and three who have given me inspiration through their recorded words and deeds.

Leaders I Have Known

Mrs. Bart Shunantona was my seventh-grade math teacher in Wewoka, Oklahoma, in 1947. She was short and round and always wore bright clothes to enhance her bright Native American complexion. She was a no-nonsense teacher who literally pushed me and the other students to excel in mathematics. I was not her prize pupil—far from it! In fact, I hated math and practically everything that had to do with school. My world as a skinny seventh grader was centered on surviving football practice.

I was a sight to behold in a football uniform. I looked like an opened care package for the homeless. Call it growth spurt or whatever you like, but in the space of 3 summer months, I turned from an attractive, normal-sized, coordinated teacher's pet in the sixth grade (I was so smart in math that I got to dust erasers on the sidewalk once a week!) to a gangly, pimple-faced, awkward seventh grader. Changing from the best athlete to the worst in 3 months is a bitter pill to swallow for a kid driven by peer approval. I was competing with eighth and ninth graders to make the ninth-grade football team as an end. Coach Miller issued me a special uniform. Whereas others had close-fitting white practice pants; a red jersey; good-looking, well-fitting cleats; and a snug-fitting helmet, I got khaki pants with sewed-in pads, a ragged white jersey that read "Property of Wewoka Junior High," shoes that were two sizes too big with loose cleats that hurt every step, and socks that slipped to my heel. The greatest insult was an old leather helmet that was so big, every time I got hit I was looking through the ear hole!

My role as football player was blocking dummy. The first team ran a single wing offense that required four blockers to clear the way. I was placed in their way—all 6 feet 2 inches, 102 pounds of me. The shoes went one way, the helmet the other each time I stood in harm's way. After each beating, I would drag my frame home and slip in without my mother seeing the scrapes and bruises. Her response was always the same—"Well, when are you going to quit taking that abuse?" I was not about to quit and risk the ridicule of my new friends. Besides, it was all I had going for me in my life during that fall so long ago. Mrs. Shunantona was on my case for not doing my math homework and for my frequent, disruptive comments to a kid named Tommy "Lame Brain" Leamy on the next row. I was a kid who needed attention and was going about getting it my way. Mrs. Shunantona tried to reach me and appeal to my serious side, but I couldn't and wouldn't hear her. Football was on my mind.

The first game of the season was with Holdenville, and I got to suit up. My uniform was unchanged, but I was proud to be on the bench for all to see. During the first quarter, we were driving for a touchdown when Coach Miller called my name! I ran up to this god in my life and said, "Yes, Coach?" He said, "Hoyle, give your shoulder pads to Billy; his just broke." I did as ordered, but my night of pride quickly faded as I sat on the end of the bench like a plucked chicken with no future. The team continued to defeat and shut out all opponents. The day before the final game with the Shawnee Wolverines (the high school team was the Wolves), I got a red jersey with the number 9 in white on the front and back. My life was looking up because of my new identity as number 9. We were clobbering Shawnee, and everyone had played but me. With 20 seconds to go in the game, Coach Miller yelled, "Hoyle, get in there at left end." I grabbed my big helmet and must have been singing "One Moment in Time" as I raced toward the huddle. As I neared my destination, my left toe caught my right heel and the rest is a blur. My helmet went spinning across the field and I crawled to recapture it. Just as I stood up with the helmet in place, I heard a gun fire. "Game's over," screamed the referee. I looked around toward the stands, which must have held 50,000 fans— well, at least 250. I saw Grandmother, Mother, Dad, snotty-nosed classmates who would give me grief, and my girlfriend Jean. Every person who counted in my seventh-grade life saw my defining moment on that football field that night. I was destroyed with no hope of repair. Should I run away from home or merely disappear into thin air?

The next morning, Mother woke me and told me to get ready for school. After I told her I was not going and that I was sick, she urged me, "Get up and I will iron your jeans the way you like them, and your favorite shirt is clean." I remained under the covers in my cocoon, refusing to reenter the world. After two more calls and no response, Mother brought the switch, and I got up and went to school and to Mrs. Shunantona's math class. I recall entering her classroom just like it was yesterday. I walked in head down, watching my big feet to avoid tripping on a desk and hurrying to find my place. Just as I was preparing to sit down, Mrs. Shunantona said, "John, you had a hard time in that football game last night, didn't you?" "Yes, ma'am," I replied. I said to myself, "Go ahead and kill me by telling the class what a failure I am." In a loud voice that still rings in my ears, she said, "Boys and girls, before we start the math lesson, listen up; I saw John Hoyle play first base on the junior police team last summer and I believe he is the best first baseman I have ever seen. Please be seated, John." My life was saved by this leader. I was so lifted that I would have tackled calculus and trigonometry that day if Mrs. Shunantona asked me to. I became her best math student by year's end and had a new handle on my self-esteem. In 2 years, I made the first team in football and made my grades. Three years later, I received a full baseball scholarship to attend Texas A&M University, and I passed freshman algebra. A great leader, Mrs. Bart Shunantona had the vision and the compassion to do the right thing at the right time to inspire me in that classroom in 1947.

Another hero and great leader in my life was Dr. Paul R. Hensarling. Dr. Hensarling was the leader I needed at a key stage in my professional development. I was a junior high science teacher and coach in Odessa, Texas, when I was awarded a National Science Foundation grant to attend a summer institute for science teachers at Texas A&M University in 1960. While taking science classes that summer, I was told about a dynamic professor over in education that I should meet. I did, and before our visit was over, my decision to major in educational administration was made. This man, Dr. Hensarling, was a salesman for the profession. He told me that day that "education needs people like you, John. Science is important, but people and their education is where the action will be in the next 25 years." How right he was, and the pride he wore as an educator was something I wanted.

I earned a master's in education, and with Dr. Hensarling as my committee chair, I was encouraged to begin a doctorate in education. With his encouragement, the following summer I resigned a well-paid administrative job in Midland, Texas, and enrolled in the doctoral program at Colorado University. I struggled to prove that I belonged in the program and tried to make ends meet, and then Dr. Hensarling entered my life once more. I received a telegram inviting me to be one of six students to initiate a new doctoral program in education at Texas A&M University. He offered an assistantship of $200 per month and had arranged for my wife to interview for a teaching job in the Bryan, Texas, schools. That telegram caused me to load my wife Carolyn, son John, Jr., daughter Laura Leigh, and dog Tippy in the car and pull a U-Haul trailer back to College Station, Texas, and enter the new Ph.D. program in education at Texas A&M University for the fall semester of 1964.

Dr. Hensarling mentored me through the program, which included an appointment to teach an undergraduate class in educational psychology. He observed my teaching and made many helpful suggestions to improve my classroom effectiveness. At one point during those three long and arduous years, I thought about quitting and finding a real job because my wife had no new clothes, our car was wearing out, and my self-esteem was tumbling. When I informed Dr. Hensarling of my thoughts of quitting the program, he looked at me a moment and responded with words that remain indelible in my mind. He said, "John, you have no idea how talented you are. Remember, just be better than you think you can be." That's all he said. I stood up, shook his hand, and left his office with a resolve to live up to his words.

Paul Hensarling had a distinguished career as a teacher, coach, principal, and superintendent before becoming a professor and department head at Texas A&M University. He knew more people than any man I had met at that point in my life. He built the department of education and psychology from a four-man department to one with more than 30 members before his retirement in 1976. During his career, he was a chief architect in the creation of the College of Education and led in the creation of the doctoral program. He is remembered throughout the state of Texas for powerful speeches and practical writings to help practicing school leaders succeed in their jobs. He brought to the professorship the combination of human compassion, keen intellect, and outstanding communication skills. His former students call Paul Hensarling the person who had the greatest impact on their personal and professional lives. He always sought perfection in himself, and graduate students knew they could do no less.

It is perhaps impossible to identify one event or person that determined one's career and accomplishments; however, Dr. Hensarling was a powerful leader in my life. He had a vision for education and for each of his students that was compelling and exciting. During his last year, Dr. Hensarling was a recipient of the Distinguished Service Award from the American Association of School Administrators. The award was presented on February 24, 1984. He received a plaque and a book titled *A Place Called School* by John Goodlad. Dr. Hensarling gave that book to me on July 30, and he died on September 3, 1984. I had not looked at the book he gave me until several weeks after his death. I opened the front cover and found the following inscription, "For my good friend's personal library—for sharing with others—Dr. John R. Hoyle, who over a lifetime has done more for me than anyone else, professionally and personally. There is no way to repay such deeds—they are part of the nature of John Hoyle. Sincerely Paul R. Hensarling." I cried as I read those words because he once again challenged me to try to "be better than you think you can be."

A third leader I have known and a name more widely known in education is Paul B. Salmon, former Executive Director of the American Association of School Administrators. Dr. Salmon served with distinction as Executive Director of AASA from 1971 until May 1985. A graduate of Whittier College, he had majors in elementary education and history and was an outstanding football player. After graduation, he taught seventh grade in Whittier, California, and then joined the U.S. Navy during World War II. His exceptional leadership capacities were identified early in his education career when he moved from a classroom teaching post to superintendent of Bloomfield School District in Artesia, California. After serving as superintendent of schools in Covina-Valley Unified School District, he moved to Pasadena, California, and then on to Sacramento in 1968. His selection as AASA Executive Director in 1971 placed him in the national spotlight in education. During the next 16 years, Paul was in the forefront of educational reform efforts nationwide and became the spokesperson for school leaders around the world in the areas of school organization and leadership. He was highly visible on Capitol Hill when education legislation and child welfare issues were under review. His commanding presence around legislators came from both his physical size—he stood 6 feet 3 inches and weighed 250 pounds—and his booming and articulate voice. He was in demand to appear on the "Today Show," the "MacNeil-Lehrer Report," and Public Broadcasting's "Latenight," and he made many appearances on local television programs discussing current problems of education.

Among his honors was the Honorary Doctor of Humane Letters from Whittier College in 1984. He was a Distinguished Professor of the National Academy for School Executives and was a frequent writer for news outlets and for major journals in education.

He traveled the country, working with school administrators and giving keynote speeches in all 50 states and around the world. His high energy and enthusiasm for public education lifted spirits and provided needed advice for school boards and superintendents engaged in school improvement. His belief in building collaboration between practitioners and professors led to several lasting changes in the preparation and practice of school leaders. He initiated the Higher Education Advisory Committee, composed of AASA members who were in professorships or university administrative positions. The committee created programs that have had a major impact on research and best practice in American education. One product of the committee is the AASA Professor of the Year, which includes a stipend for a respected professor to spend 3 months in Arlington, Virginia, at AASA as a scholar in residence. I was selected for the award in 1982, where, during the first 2 weeks, Dr. Salmon asked me to facilitate a project to develop a set of guidelines for the preparation of school administrators. The guidelines were completed in October 1982 and became the first national benchmarks for the preparation and professional development of principals and superintendents. The guidelines led to the publication of a widely used textbook, *Skills for Successful School Leaders* (Hoyle, English, & Steffy, 1985). The second edition was completed in 1990 and revised in 1994. Other projects that Paul Salmon inspired were recognition for outstanding university preparation programs and additional activities to bring university and public school leaders together.

The attribute that set Paul Salmon on a special level, and the reason that he is in this book, is that he always asked administrators, project directors, and others if children would truly benefit from their plan and project. In 1982, when Paul charged me to write the guidelines, I spent many long nights conducting research and writing. Each morning, Paul would scrutinize the draft, look up under bushy eyebrows, and ask, "Where are the kids in this?" Back

I went to rewrite what I thought was already a masterpiece. After several rejections of portions of the manuscript, he declared it fit for submission to the AASA Executive Committee for their review and approval. Students and their needs are prominent in each of the skills and competencies in the document. Completed in 1982, the guidelines became a guide for the majority of the preparation programs in the United States. The eight skill areas in the guidelines were the foundation for the Professional Standards for the Superintendency published by AASA in 1993.

Paul B. Salmon retired from AASA on March 31, 1985, and began a speaking and consulting career to share his vision and energy across America. His life and exciting career were cut short by a Delta Airline disaster in Dallas, Texas, on July 16, 1985. This accident was a tragedy not only for Paul's family and friends but for education as well. His dynamic personality, powerful persuasive voice, and tireless energy could not be replaced. However, his legacy lives on in the students he taught, the administrators he prepared, the education legislation he influenced, and the positive image he maintained for those around him. Paul exemplifies the characteristics of outstanding leaders found in the leadership research and in the conversations about the mystique of those we want to follow.

These leaders I knew and respected. Each of the three, Mrs. Shunantona, Dr. Hensarling, and Dr. Salmon, were unique leaders with many winning attributes. Two were not national figures; one was. One was a Native American teacher in a small Oklahoma town, one was a professor in a major university, and one directed a national professional administrator association with over 18,000 members. What, then, were the common leadership characteristics that marked their journey through my life? Three characteristics come to mind: capacity for caring for others, clear communication, and a commitment to persist.

They were each very active, busy people with limited time to spare, but they found the time for me. I could have left Mrs. Shunantona's life with a hatred for math and for teachers in general, but she had a vision for me and her other students. Paul Hensarling could have ignored my whining as just a stage of graduate school, but he listened and used the right words at the right time to keep me moving toward my goal. Paul Salmon, in his lofty position, could have been too busy to ask me to attempt to develop a set of preparation guidelines or to critique each line looking for the "kids." The capacity to care for me and hundreds of others is the first ingredient of the makeup of these three idols of mine.

There was never any need to hire an interpreter to explain anything my three leaders said. Mrs. Shunantona knew the right words and expressions to build a fire in me to succeed. Paul Hensarling's words were positive and challenging as he spoke them or wrote them in professional journals. His penmanship was an art form, and his words, even those spoken in a whisper in his last few days, were as clear as a late summer sky. Paul Salmon was a master with a phrase and didn't mind correcting me if he detected an improper use of a word. He once nailed me for using "irregardless" and another person for using "hopefully" in the wrong way. He believed that the words a person used were the window to his or her character. The correct word in the right place at the right time from these leaders left an indelible impression on me and others.

These three leaders never gave up. Mrs. Shunantona refused to let me or any other student give up. Failure was not in her vocabulary when it came to her students. She spent more than 40 years telling the same story to all of her students and their parents. She left in me a drive to finish what I start.

Dr. Hensarling was a master at making the routine of starting the same class each semester or planning the annual superintendent conference appear to be fresh and exciting. He never tired of doing the same things because he added a new wrinkle to each new semester or conference. Also, his extraordinary skill of listening to the woes of burned-out graduate students and faculty, and then to select the right words to give them a renewed spirit, were marks of a gifted leader.

Dr. Salmon was a bulldog at seeing a job through to completion. He could hold his own with the most persuasive politician on Capitol Hill or with critics of public schools. He believed that persistence loaded with good data could win most battles for education and the children of America's schools. Dr. Salmon was the one person educators wanted on their side in a debate on any educational policy matter. You knew he would never "cut and run" when the battle began.

Thus the capacity for caring for others, the ability to communicate with clear meaning, and a commitment to persist defined these three great leaders. You, the reader, can no doubt select leaders from your past who also possess these and other attributes. Although the literature on leadership is pregnant with lists of attributes and characteristics of leaders, it is important to remember those who didn't need a list to guide them in the complex roles they played as leaders. These real people facing real-world problems ran the complete race of leadership. Throughout the remainder of this book, I will refer to the three leaders that I knew and to the three great leaders of history that I did not know, but wish I had.

Leaders I Wish I Had Known

The following leaders of history have intrigued me for many years. I have often wondered what it would have been like to have engaged these giants in conversation about leadership and the skills they each used to inspire ordinary people to extraordinary accomplishments. I have chosen Jesus of Nazareth, Joan of Arc, and Winston Spencer Churchill as the leaders I would like to have known.

Jesus, or Jesus the Christ, is certainly a well-known figure. The written accounts of his leadership accomplishments are found in the four Gospels of Matthew, Mark, Luke, and John, and the epistles of the New Testament. Even though the facts of Jesus's career are subject to question, and many traditional sayings ascribed to Jesus are unreliable, his larger-than-life influence has had a major impact on the course of human history.

Very little is known about his childhood and youth in terms of formal education. The scriptures recorded his baptism by his cousin John the Baptist and his time of meditation and solitude before beginning a 3-year ministry. This 3-year ministry included profound teachings using the language of the common people of the day. He reached out to the oppressed, to children, and to the ill and outcast of society. The scriptures tell of miracle cures and revolutionary ideas that caught the eyes of the Pharisees and scribes. This ruling clique decided to eliminate Jesus, whom they considered a revolutionary leader and violent reformer. He was arrested, convicted of crimes carrying the death penalty in Jewish law, and turned over to the Romans to carry out the sentence. Charged with treason against Rome, Pilate delivered Jesus to be crucified. According to the scriptures, 3 days later, an angel told visitors to his grave that he had risen from the dead. Later, he was seen by his disciples before ascending into heaven.

Writers, artists, musicians, and others have long been inspired by the incidents in the life of Jesus. Brooks (1956) wrote about the leadership of Jesus, saying,

> He never traveled more than 200 miles from home, never wrote a book, never earned a college degree, but all of the governments that ever sat, all of the armies that ever marched, all the navies that ever sailed have not had the impact on history of this solitary life. (p. 45)

Jesus of Nazareth also displayed the three characteristics of the three leaders I knew personally. He had a deep and profound sense of caring for others, especially those unable to help themselves. He used the common language of the day and used parables to communicate clear messages to all who listened. His message was so clear and persuasive that individuals dropped what they were doing and followed Him. Clearly, Jesus had a commitment to persist even unto death. He died for his cause to lift the human race to one of compassion and equity for all races and creeds.[1]

Joan of Arc is a French saint and national heroine who through her charisma and determination almost succeeded in chasing the English forces from French soil. Born in Domremy, France, in 1412, she began to hear the voices of three saints early in her life in her garden in Domremy. Inspired by these voices, Joan of Arc convinced the authorities that she could lead troops and win in battle to lift the siege of Orleans and other English-held encampments along the Loire river. She then convinced Charles VII to march on Rheims, where he was crowned in her presence. King Charles and his close advisors slowed the military progress of Joan and her armies by negotiating with Burgundy, England's independent ally, who later captured her at the battle of Compiègne and sold her to the English.

Her trial in Rouen was an effort to force her to recant the "voices" that convinced her to place her faith in God over the church hierarchy and to end her quest to lead soldiers in battle against the English. She refused and was condemned for heresy and sorcery. In 1431, she was burned at the stake. A later trial in 1456 reversed the decision and praised her for inspiring her country in a time of English conquest. She was canonized a saint in 1920.

Historians are in general agreement about the leadership style of Joan of Arc. She was inspired by her faith to lead in battle, and she led with spear in hand without a helmet for protection to enable her soldiers to see her long blonde hair. At the siege of Orleans, she was severely wounded in the shoulder by a spear. She was assisted in removing the spear and rallied her men to continue the battle. This inspired them to continue fighting and to take Orleans. Her capacity of caring for her beloved France and her people led Joan of Arc to convince the Dauphin and others at Chinon to give her an army. She was a master communicator to her superiors, to soldiers, and to the people of France to persuade them to follow her in this noble cause. Her commitment to persist against the English-controlled court of law that conducted her irregular and biased trial and to stay true to her beliefs in the face of death is a testimony to her values of truth and determination. The judge for the trial was an ambitious bishop named Pierre Cauchon, who was a pawn of the English and conducted a trial that was later found to be an injustice. In 1456, Pope Calixtus III declared Joan's name forever cleansed of all charges against it (Banfield, 1985).

Her leadership has been an inspiration for some of the world's artists, military leaders, and writers. Banfield (1985) said,

> Thousands of people still turn to Joan's story daily, from the soldier of whom great bravery is required to the young girl who needs the quiet courage to be honest with her lover. In this brief but so-powerful life they find the help they need to remain true, through whatever arises, to the voice within them. (p. 107)[2]

One of the world's most revered statesmen, military strategists, orators, and charismatic leaders of the 20th century, Winston Churchill inspired his compatriots to fight on against tremendous odds in World War II. Born into nobility and wealth, Churchill was a problem child and poor student. He lived a checkered childhood full of mischief, school failure, and heartache for his parents, who were too busy to give him a happy home and childhood. Churchill spent the rest of his life trying to make his father proud of him.

After a lackluster record in several schools, he entered the Royal Military Academy at Sandhurst, where he became a serious student of literature and military science. At age 16, he revealed his visionary prowess when he went to see the family doctor about a speech impediment—a slight lisp. The doctor told him to forget about the lisp because as a soldier, he would not be a speaker but a fighter. Churchill reputedly responded that he would someday become a great statesman like his father and that "I must be able to make an important speech without worrying that I cannot say the letter 's' " (Rogers, 1986, p. 25). His powerful, persuasive speeches became his trademark as a leader. He started his path to power by becoming a war correspondent and soldier to gain fame and recognition so that he could enter public office like his father. His writings caught the public's attention early. His first book about the war against the native tribesmen of India, titled *The Story of Malakand Field Force*, was widely read and was the first of many volumes on war, politics, and his life. After escaping from the enemy during the Boer War, Churchill became a national celebrity. This fame led to his election to Parliament and to more than 50 years of public service to his country.

He met both success and failure during his long and storied career. During World War I, he was forced to resign as First Lord of the Admiralty because of the decisions he made that led indirectly to the disaster at Gallipoli. He lost his seat in Parliament in 1921, but was reelected in 1924. He began warning the world about the increasing aggression of the new German leader, Adolf Hitler, in 1932, but he had few listeners until it was almost too late. Appointed Prime Minister a year after Britain declared war against Germany, he became a man of destiny for his country. After his appointment, his words before the House of Commons became among his most famous: "I have nothing to offer but blood, toil, tears, and sweat; you ask what is our aim? I can answer in one word: Victory—victory in spite of all terror" (Rogers, 1986, p. 75). Later, during one of the darkest hours of the war, he galvanized his people when he said, "We shall not flag or fail. We shall go the end. We shall fight in France, we shall fight on the seas and oceans, we shall fight with growing confidence and growing strength in the air, we shall defend our island whatever the cost may be" (Rogers, 1986, p. 77). He was a master with words at the right time throughout his career. Speaking before the House of Commons on June 18, 1940, Churchill said, "Let us therefore brace ourselves, that if the British Empire and its Commonwealth last for a thousand years, men will still say, 'This was their finest hour' " (Rogers, 1986, p. 75).

But he was also known for his biting wit. A story is told about Churchill and Lady Astor, a very dignified lady of wealth, sitting next to each other at a dinner party. She said, "Winston, if I were your wife, I'd poison your soup." He replied, "Nancy, if I were your husband, I'd drink it" (Manchester, 1983, p. 34).

Churchill was a man of tenacity. He continued when lesser persons would have changed careers. After inspiring the British people and the world to help defeat the German and Italian forces, his party lost in the elections of 1945, and he lost his post as prime minister because the people wanted to go in a new, more liberal direction. He continued his speaking and writing and positive approach, and he returned to office as Prime Minister following the Conservative election victory in 1951. Invested Knight of the Garter by Queen Elizabeth II in 1953, he later won the Nobel Prize for literature. A master of the quip, during his final year of life he said, "I'm ready to meet my maker, whether my maker is prepared for the great ordeal of meeting me is another matter" (Rogers, 1986, p. 107). A visionary and humorist to the end, Winston Churchill was a great man for his time and for his beloved England (Rogers, 1986).

Churchill clearly fits within my three characteristics of capacity for caring for others, communicating clear meaning, and commitment to persist. His love for the people of his country in peace and war marked his life, and his speeches and writing are among the most long remembered. His "victory" speech sums up his commit-

All the leaders discussed in this book—Mrs. Shunantona, Paul Hensarling, Paul Salmon, Jesus, Joan of Arc, Winston Churchill—had the characteristics shown in the following list. Give yourself one point for each item listed, then show your total at the bottom (19 is a perfect score). How do *you* measure up?

Characteristic	You
Caring	___
Communicator	___
Listener	___
Persuader	___
Persistent	___
Visionary	___
Optimistic	___
Energetic (Fit)	___
Humorous	___
Creative	___
Tolerant	___
Patient	___
Learner	___
Mixer	___
Mediator	___
Collaborator	___
Gentle	___
Consistent	___
Honest	___
Total	___

Figure 1.1. Leadership Comparison Checklist

ment to persist when others had given up. His vision was toward a better day for England and the price it took to gain it.[3]

These six leaders—three of whom I knew and three I wish I had known—are the inspiration and context of this book. Each of these special personalities moved people and programs to success. By their character, wisdom, and vision, they led others to find their own inner greatness. Arthur M. Schlesinger Jr. captured the essence of the influence of great leaders when he wrote, "The signal benefit the great leaders confer is to embolden the rest of us to live

according to our own best selves, to be active, insistent, and reso-
lute in affirming our own sense of things. . . . And they attest to the
wisdom and power that may lie within the most unlikely of us"
(Rogers, 1986, p. 9).

While conducting research on visioning leadership, I revisited
the lives and accomplishments of several prominent leaders other
than those six I selected for this chapter. Among them were
Mahatma Gandhi, John F. Kennedy, Martin Luther King Jr., Florence
Nightingale, and Abraham Lincoln. These remarkable leaders
were unique personalities who could "embolden the rest of us to
live according to our own best selves." Out of their uniqueness
came a consistent set of characteristics or leadership attributes that
provide help for others who wish to become visionary leaders. Figure 1.1 is a list of 19 of those attributes that the reader can use to
compare his or her leadership qualities. If you have attained a perfect score of 19, you may stop reading the book now!

In the following four chapters, the reader will be reminded of
these great leaders and the attributes they possessed. I hope that
you, the reader, will recall great leaders in your life and reflect how
their influence on you has challenged you to "be better than you
think you can be."

Notes

1. Details in the life of Jesus were selected from the *Columbia Viking Desk Encyclo-
pedia*, published by The Viking Press, New York, 1953.
2. The primary source for the life of Joan of Arc was *Joan of Arc* by S. Banfield,
1985, New York: Chelsea House.
3. The primary source for the life of Winston Churchill was *Winston Churchill* by
J. Rogers, 1986, New York: Chelsea House.

Futuring and Motivating Others Through the Art of Persuasion

G reat leaders have a knack for inventing their own future. They literally experience their victories or accomplishments in their minds long before they actually occur. The art and science of the study of futurism, futuristics, and future studies has emerged as a respected field of inquiry in universities, corporations, government, agriculture, and other organizations. The search for a more successful tomorrow is the quest of most humans, and the need to anticipate and manage a brighter future is a universal need.

Future studies has grown from isolated groups of social scientists and artists to widespread interest and organized groups, such as the World Future Society, with over 40,000 members. This global interest has moved futurism from the image of fortune-telling, palm reading, and crystal balls to sophisticated trend analysis, scenario activities, and computer-driven data sets used to compile alternative scenarios on almost any topic. Although futurists do not attempt to predict the future, they can design preferred, or most likely, futures that fall within certain guidelines.

According to Edward Cornish, editor of the journal *Futurist,* those who study the future concentrate on three key areas. One, they believe that the world and all of its systems and inhabitants are interconnected and thus dependent on each other for survival. Two, futurists are focused on time as a critical force. They believe that to change the course of events, one begins now, not next week or next month. The future of the environment, the quality of the air, water, food supply, and human interactions is not determined in 5 years but now! Three, ideas of the future or the skill of futuring is paramount for improving the lot of humankind. Imagining a university, school, or food system where all people are well educated, fed nutritionally, clothed, and housed in safe, comfortable communities are examples of ideas for the future.

Based on these three areas, futurists strive to anticipate what will occur. Some events are simpler to forecast than others. For instance, demographics are easier because data are accessible on world population trends and on those already here. At the current rate and fertility data, the world population increases at 2.8 births per second and 242,000 each week. Currently, the global population is 5.6 billion. Although the population growth has slowed down somewhat because of decreasing fertility rates, the numbers keep rising. The projections for 2025 range from 7.6 to 9.4 billion, depending upon several factors (Bishop, 1994). By 2025, the population of Africa will be three times that of Europe (1.58 billion vs. 512 million). Behind these alarming statistics lies the reality: Each human being requires daily 2,000 to 3,000 calories and 4½ pounds of water. Obviously, this need is not being met in many troubling spots in the world today (Kennedy, 1993). Other trends in economics, technology, agriculture, medicine, and human morality remain very difficult areas to forecast. Because 80% of the new technologies necessary to compete in world markets have not been discovered, no one data set or scenario is adequate to grab a vision of the future. Thus the study of the future is a tool to manage change or at least be able to adjust to it.

If leaders are to earn followers, then they must model ways to create the future rather than suffer its consequences. King Solomon is credited with saying, "A prudent man foresees the difficulties ahead and prepares for them. The simpleton goes blindly on and suffers the consequences." Therefore, to get a better feel of the future, we must make some assumptions about how future studies can guide our visioning.

Assumption #1

To affect the future, we must begin now. It is impossible to change course on a roller coaster because about all we can do is hang on until it completes its course. We must assume that we can change our course as a captain would steer a boat to the harbor or down a rapidly moving river. Change must occur early if the boat is to arrive safely at the mouth of the river. We are often tied to a successful past, and when trouble strikes, we are unprepared to make changes in time to avoid running aground.

Assumption #2

Because there are usually alternative futures, it is impossible to know which one will happen; they all could happen. We must remain flexible about the number of assumptions we consider because false assumptions can lead in the wrong direction. It is wise to consider both the pessimistic and the optimistic alternatives to avoid pitfalls along the way.

Assumption #3

Before agreeing on a preferred future course of action, engage others who must make the future happen. A vision that is clear to the leader may be a dense fog to others in the organization. An alternative future that is owned only by the leader is doomed to failure unless it is seen and felt by those who must help the vision happen. When Lee Iacocca turned around the Chrysler Corporation, he felt in his bones that the K car and family vans were the future, and he went about convincing stockholders and the government, which helped to bail Chrysler out of deep financial trouble. Then he convinced the buying public (Bishop, 1994).

What Is Futuring Anyway?

Futuring is the act of seeing and feeling alternative futures that are either in the near (5 to 10 years), middle (11 to 20 years), or far (21 to 50 years) future. The act of futuring can be done by individuals or groups depending on the need. The futuring process begins with an idea or belief that can range from the probable or realistic to the improbable or unrealistic.

The terms *futuring* and *visioning* are used interchangeably in the literature and in this book. Futuring or visioning helps individuals and organizations create desired futures that give a compelling future pull or focus. A vision is often spoken by leaders, but it must be shared by others if the vision is to be realized (Bishop, 1994). Futurist Joel Barker, in the video titled *The Power of Vision,* believes that a vision community must be created through a visionary, energetic leader who influences followers to share and support the vision. Next, the followers help construct detailed and comprehensive plans that are perceived to be inspiring and worth their efforts. When this occurs, the vision community is empowered to make the vision happen.

Vision Statement

A written vision statement is the inspiration to drive an idea. It is different from a mission statement and goals. A vision statement is created and shared by members or clients within the organization to inspire their future efforts. The statement should be brief, simple, and above all else, inspiring.

Mission Statement

A mission statement is developed by the group to explain to external members or clients what the organization does and how it carries out its tasks. The mission statement is more detailed than the vision statement because it should include multiple missions and processes for the customers or clients.

Figure 2.1. The Three Essential Elements for Making Visions Happen

Goal Statement

Goal statements are the detailed, specific statements directed at accomplishing the mission(s) and are guided by the vision. Goal statements include the more specific objectives or enablers that lead the group or individuals to goal accomplishments. (See Figure 2.1.)

If a vision is to drive the mission and goals, then it should be realistic, attractive, and imaginative. However, unless a careful study of trends and issues is conducted and the assumptions upon which the vision is based are sound, fantasy may rule over reality (Bishop, 1994).

The reader can determine if the following scenario developed by a high school junior is realistic or not. His scenario was the end result of a futuring exercise for a class of gifted juniors and seniors. I was invited to conduct a workshop for the class and noticed that all of the students looked "gifted" except for one small Hispanic boy. I knew what gifted kids looked like because they wore wire on their teeth and horses on their shirts. Is there a connection between wealth and students chosen for classes for the gifted and talented? Anyway, I asked the teacher about the young lad and she told me that he was a creative thinker and terrific young man who was being raised by his grandparents because he had been abandoned as an infant. The teacher said, "Besides that, these other so-called gifted kids needed to see what real giftedness was all about." I told the students to write their future in the form of a scenario and provide a copy for me in the next 2 weeks. I was expecially interested in reading what this "different kid" would write. In 2 weeks, the class compilation of scenarios arrived and I anxiously thumbed through to find his effort. He created his future in the following piece.

My name is _____, and it is now 2015, and I am sitting on the fourth deck of the Kyle Field football stadium at Texas A&M University watching a game between the Aggies and the Texas Longhorns. I am proud of this fourth deck since I built it two years ago to help accommodate 90,000 fans who wish to follow their national powerhouse team. I not only built this deck, but also built a geodesic dome over the entire campus to preserve the buildings from the acid rain from the air pollution caused by extended use of fossil fuels and to maintain a climate controlled educational environment. Oh, hold it for a second while I use my instant replay binoculars to look at that last play—stupid referee missed another call! I designed these binoculars in 1998 and became an instant millionaire. After completing high school, I entered Texas A&M University and earned degrees in architecture and engineering and went to work for a large engineering firm for two years. After two boring and unchallenging years playing the corporate loyalty, non-risk game, I stole their best ideas and formed my own company. I guess you would call me an entrepreneur. I hired several imaginative risk-takers and the results have been remarkable. My group can create a new town in three weeks in practically any spot on earth; we are growing food on the ocean floor and in outer space; we can literally feed the hungry of the world and provide health care to third world nations and resources for improved educational opportunity for all urban and rural poor children. Along the way in 1995 I received a law degree from the University of Texas to help me deal with the litigious society of the time. I am pleased with my life and the capability to help others less fortunate. I plan to move into the housing industry soon and eliminate the slums and tenant housing throughout this country. Much remains to be done, but with hard work and a vision of success, I shall prevail.

Twelve years after that scenario was composed, I ran into the teacher who invited me on that day. When inquiring about the young man who wrote that fascinating scenario, she replied, "Haven't you heard, he recently completed his law degree at the University of Texas!" I shouted, "Go find him!" The teacher looked puzzled at my enthusiastic response and asked why I wanted to know of her former student's whereabouts. I said, "I want a ticket so that I can sit next to him for that football game against the Texas Longhorns in the fall of 2015!" I have not talked to him nor do I plan to, but how much of his future will he make happen? Perhaps he has an alternate plan just in case he fails to reach his preferred future. It is obvious that he began his journey toward his desired future very early and in earnest. There are lessons to be learned from this enterprising visionary who is a master at imagineering, or creating his future.

Futuring and Intuition

Futuring and intuition have similar characteristics. According to Roy Rowan (1986), author of *The Intuitive Manager,*

> Intuition is knowledge gained without rational thought. And since it comes from some stratum of awareness just below the conscious level, it is slippery and elusive, to say the least. . . . New ideals spring from a mind that organizes experiences, facts, and relationships to discern a path that has not been taken before. Somewhere along this uncharted path, intuition compresses years of learning and experience into an instantaneous flash. (pp. 11,12)

Futuring is similar to intuition in many ways because imagination is a key variable to creating preferred futures. Eugene Raudsepp, a specialist on intuition and daydreaming to dream up successful futures, believes that we can engineer our own future by picturing ourselves as we want to become or accomplishing what we want. He believes that we must picture these desired objectives as if we had already attained them. The U.S. ice hockey team that won the

1980 Olympic gold medal did the impossible by beating the Soviet Union. The millions of fans watching went crazy with joy over the victory while a television announcer was trying to interview one of the victorious players. When asked if this was the happiest day of his life, the player replied, "Not really. You see, the team had already celebrated this victory many times over in practice. We envisioned winning the match against the Soviet Union and having the gold medal placed around our necks after each victory. Our coach would then tell us that since we were now gold medal winners, go out today and play like champions." This approach to futuring is vital because the individual or group must feel as well as see the desirability of structuring a desirable future.

Futuring does rely on good data and a sound knowledge of global trends and sources of change. A grasp of the latest developments in technology, government, economics, education, medicine and health, agriculture, and demographics are examples of the areas that need close attention to "ramp up" or prepare for successful futuring activities.

Futuring involves a wide range of knowledge and skills in visioning. The "vision thing" is thrown about with reckless abandon and can lose its power as a result. Visions are a lot like love or beauty—we know them when we see or feel them, but their definitions are difficult. Some people, such as Lee Iacocca, Steve Jobs, and Jack Welch, have vision. Others may never have it no matter how hard they try. People tend to limit themselves and fail to achieve their dreams because they limit their vision. In the same vein, an old track coach told his athlete, "Never build hurdles in your mind, because the hurdles on the track are much smaller than the hurdles in the mind." And there is much truth in the words of consultant Jim Huge who said, "If you believe you can or you can't, you are right either way."

Futuring and Leaders

Leaders of schools and other learning organizations who seek to improve their futuring skills and vision can learn valuable lessons from the visionaries of history. Earlier, I described how Joan of Arc had a vision to inspire her armies to chase the British from French soil. Her vision did not include treachery by Charles VII and others that led to her demise. Galileo's visions and astronomical discoveries confirmed Copernicus's theory of the solar system, but he was forced by church authorities with other visions to recant his belief that the Earth moved around the sun. John F. Kennedy's vision led Neil Armstrong to step on the moon and exclaim, "One small step for man, one giant leap for mankind." Unfortunately, Kennedy didn't live to see his dream become a reality.

Futuring is an exciting process to move people to imagine new and challenging opportunities for students and other clients in a learning organization. The future will not be a repeat of the past, nor will the future be any more predictable in 10 years. The past will never catch the future and become the "good old days." The good old days exist only in our minds, and few of us would return to them if we had the chance. As Yogi Berra said, "The future ain't what it used to be."

The most important ingredient in the futuring recipe is the enthusiasm and vision by the formal leader of the organization. If the leader is excited about creating opportunities for all learners and a better, more productive existence for all students touched by the school or system, then others may also catch the enthusiasm. Remember, "You can't light a fire with a wet match."

Motivating Others to Engage in Futuring

"Oh, no, not another meeting where we sit around and contemplate our navels," moaned a colleague about a special meeting. Most professionals are sick and tired of appeasing the boss and listening to him or her talk about a new "gee whiz" reform strategy. People have been bombarded with movements such as quality circles, strategic planning, effective schools, total quality management, and site-based decision making. Teachers and agency professionals have been assigned to groups to set goals, plan curricula, align curricula, and select personnel, only to be told after 6 months of meetings that the decision that the committee recommended to superiors must be overruled because of a new mandate, a lack of funds, or the superiors' decision that a different direction is needed. When administrators bemoan that "my staff is apathetic or belligerent to this new plan," it is an indication that no foundation for collaboration has been built and the trust level is low. What can a leader do to make a personal vision become a group, school, or system vision?

One method is to create enthusiasm for a cause beyond oneself. When the leader is attempting to build a fire under the staff to look at an idea or vision, he or she must focus on the student or client. A visual of a "generic kid" (a smiley face with big eyes and a sprig of hair) is one example to help the group center on the reason for their existence in the first place. The notion of the generic kid or client should lead to the discussion of inclusion, not exclusion, of all children or clients. It is vital to remind the group that servant leadership is the style to model and to remember that what each group member wishes for his or her child is what should be wished for every child in the system. Mrs. Shunantona expected the same high performance from me in math and in football that she expected from her son Richard, who was a starting end and captain of that Wewoka Junior High team in 1947. Paul Salmon expected every member of the American Association of School Administrators to treat each student the same—with respect and the greatest possible support to help the child be a caring, productive, global citizen. The customer is not always right, but the job of the leader is to inspire others to create schools and programs that will offer the customer alternative paths to success.

Telling an inspirational story about people who fought for a cause beyond themselves is a good way to increase group commitment. Hazel Brannen Smith, a journalist, had a dream to return to her hometown in rural Mississippi in 1954 and start a newspaper that would take a different direction in editorial writing. She began writing editorials about healing Black and White relationships and encouraging people to work together to improve schools and the community. She suggested that this would help the town prosper and offer brighter futures for their children. However, Hazel Smith had forgotten how deeply rooted the racial hatred was among certain individuals. She received physical threats from business owners, who pulled their advertising dollars from her paper. Lifelong friends ostracized her, her husband died in an accident, and her newspaper building was burned to the ground. This small dynamo of a woman held on to her vision, and a handful of loyal employees stayed by her side while she went elsewhere to borrow money to reopen her newspaper. Another newspaper was begun in an attempt to thwart her efforts to resurrect her paper and to solicit the local advertising dollar. Undaunted, Hazel Brannen Smith reopened her paper and continued her editorial writing. Her words began to open some closed minds and the community began to tolerate her, and later she found more acceptance by those who had turned their backs on her. Her persistence paid off and the community grew to be much more tolerant and inclusive in educational and community programs. Her gallantry and the drive to turn a vision into a reality led to national recognition. In 1964, Hazel Brannen Smith became the first woman to win a Pulitzer Prize for editorial writing. She had a vision and cause beyond herself that made her community a better place.

Designing the Future and Persuasion

Present your vision of an attractive future. If you, the leader, expect others to become engaged in designing the future, you need to show them yours—future, that is! Using data on the demographics, economy, technology, and other general trends affecting your future, create a scenario or future picture describing a learning environment in the next 15 years in which all clients are being served by caring professionals from education, agencies, government, industry, and health care. Show how the use of voice-activated computers and virtual reality technologies spark the imagination of all learners and are easily accessible. When one of Walt Disney's granddaughters visited Epcot Center in Orlando, Florida, for the first time, she exclaimed, "This is beautiful, I just wish that granddad could have seen it." Her mother said, "My dear, your grandfather did see it—he created it in his mind years ago. His vision inspired others to build it."

After creating a vision, administrators and managers need the skill of persuasion. According to George Manners and Joseph

Steger (1979), who are management scholars, persuasion is difficult to learn. Of the nine leadership and management skills they
identify, persuasion is the most difficult skill to master. Most managers agree with the research that persuasion is difficult to learn
and very difficult to apply. Most administrators do not think themselves to be persuasive and able to inspire their followers. This perception of being uninspiring persuaders does not jibe with how
they actually act when trying to make a deal or sell an idea. Kouzes
and Posner (1987) write that

> When relating our hopes, dreams, and successes, we are al-
> ways unnaturally expressive. We lean forward in our chairs,
> our arms move about, our eyes light up, our voices sing with
> emotion, and smiles appear on our faces. We are enthusiastic,
> articulate, optimistic, and uplifting. In short, we are inspiring.
> (p. 109)

In spite of the way we gesture and express enthusiasm, we remain
convinced that our skills in persuasion are weak, and we believe
that we lack the mystique that comes with being a charismatic visionary. Persuasion is difficult to learn, but its pursuit must be
never ending. Persuasion enables a leader to get people to do things
contrary to their own wishes or desires. Leaders must be able to
convince others—often those over whom they have no administrative control—to follow them in a project or idea. When speaking to
a group or a large gathering, you must get them personally involved by touching their emotions about their work, family, or personal ambitions. Create in each listener a desire to be a part of a
"cause beyond oneself" and describe specific steps to take in that
direction. If you want to persuade others, you must be sincere, enthusiastic, and honest in your remarks. You must touch the audience's hearts to turn their heads. Great leaders are remembered for
their vision and ability to spark others through the art of persuasion to join in creating the vision.

Scott Cutlip, Allen Center, and Glen Broom (1985), specialists in
public relations and the art of persuasion, offer four guiding principles that emerge from experimental research.

1. Identification Principle. Most people will ignore an idea or a point of view unless they see that it affects their personal fears, desires, hopes, or aspirations.

2. Action Principle. People seldom buy ideas separated from action—either action taken by the sponsor of the idea or action that the people themselves can conveniently take to prove the merit of the idea.

3. Principle of Familiarity and Trust. We buy ideas only from those we trust; we are influenced by, or adopt, only those opinions or points of view put forward by individuals, corporations, or institutions that we regard as credible.

4. Clarity Principle. The situation must be clear to us, not confusing. The thing we observe, read, see, or hear, the thing that produces our impressions, must be clear, not subject to several interpretations. People tend to see things as black or white. To communicate, one must employ words, symbols, or stereotypes that the receiver comprehends and responds to. (pp. 178-179)

If people view you as a person who knows what they need to grow as professionals and who can lead them in a plan for action that is both credible and clearly understood, then you are mastering the art of persuasion. Paul Salmon was a master at selling political leaders and school leaders on school reform legislation and at creating new programs for students with special needs. His powerful opposition to tax credits and school vouchers that would take money from public schools was expressed in "stump speeches" or guest opinion editorial articles in national newspapers. In one of his speeches, his words were clear and to the point:

> Tax credits for parents who plan to enroll their children in private schools are not only damaging to the public schools, but to America. If you want to build a swimming pool in your back yard, go ahead—just do not expect me to pay for it.

Persuasion can motivate people to act and begin new conversations about ways to transform teaching and learning.

Conclusions

The art of futuring is the process of analyzing numerous social and technological changes and trends that surround and affect schools and other organizations. Futuring prepares leaders to use the art of visioning to build learning environments and gives them the skills to persuade others to make the vision become a reality. Chapter 3 will concentrate on transforming visions into realities and will present a few examples of ways to create visions that should rally others to the venture.

Transforming the Vision Into Reality to Rally the Troops

If the "cause beyond oneself" and your vision have been communicated in a persuasive manner, the next step should be successful. Ralph Waldo Emerson believed in dreamers who dream big ideas, but also that these ideas must be fulfilled. Some administrators must talk about every idea for so long that they squeeze the life out of the idea. Unless the leader has the skill to capture the imagination of a group in a short time, the idea or vision will die quickly. Busy professionals protect their time, and unless their intellect and soul can be reached in a few moments, they are "out of here." If the group feels the fire in an idea and if the idea or vision is focused on each of them and their role in it, the vision is alive. The leader must breathe life into his or her vision (Kouzes & Posner, 1987). The coals of an idea must be blown into a bright flame by those who will make the vision come to pass.

An idea that grew from the battlefield of southeast Asia led to a national symbol of bravery and loyalty. In 1969, a young soldier was severely wounded by a mortar shell in Viet Nam, and several of his buddies were killed or wounded. The young soldier, Jan Scruggs, was in and out of hospitals for 3 years to repair his broken body and spirit. He endured sleepless nights because of the memories of his friends who died in that far-off hellhole in southeast Asia. Also, he was distressed that America had forgotten the price his friends had paid for their country in a controversial war, and because he didn't want the American public to forget his buddies, he decided to do something about it. He had no money and little influence to create a memorial or a fund, so he and two friends contacted members of Congress about the idea and then spent their own money to register the Viet Nam Memorial Fund. Scruggs called a news conference to announce the fund. Next, Congress set aside a piece of land near the Lincoln Memorial in Washington, DC, and gave Jan and his committee 5 years to raise the funds for the memorial. The appeal for funding caught the attention of the public, and the money was raised in 2 years. On November 12, 1982, Jan Scruggs and his buddies and friends participated in the dedication of the beautiful Viet Nam Memorial. Jan Scruggs had a vision to honor young American soldiers who gave their full measure of devotion for their country. One person, one vision, and a determination to tell an important story created a symbol of respect and beauty dedicated to his fallen friends. His persistence and the determination to enlist others caused the vision to happen (Scruggs & Swerdlow, 1985).

John Champlain had a vision to radically reform the Johnson City, New York schools in a period of 10 years. When he became superintendent in 1978, the Johnson City schools were an educational disaster. Within 5 years, Champlain led the district to some amazing results. Employing the belief that all children can learn at high levels, and by relying on Ben Bloom's mastery learning model, Champlain's first graders achieved a full grade above their grade level, and fifth graders achieved a grade and a half above their level. Students in the eighth grade and above achieved nearly 3 years above their grade level—a feat believed to be impossible!

Before 1979, only 10% of the graduates entered higher education, and 40% dropped out in the ninth grade to find jobs in the local shoe factory. John Champlain became a celebrity, with stories appearing in the *New York Times* and frequent appearances on TV talk shows. I visited the Johnson City schools in 1982 and found the test results and classroom successes to be valid. People from around the globe came to see this miracle that Champlain and his team had built. How did John Champlain take this low-achieving system and turn it around? First, he took a risk by telling the school board during the job interview of his vision, which included the goal of higher standards and achievement if the board would support him when the change process began causing some upheaval among the teaching and administrative staff. He warned them that he would need money to help carry out his vision. The board was so desperate for some successes that they hired Champlain and promised their support. During the first year, Champlain told his vision over and over to all who would listen in the hope of attracting a few devotees to his cause. A handful of teachers and administrators came aboard, and Champlain conducted the staff development himself and invited others to attend. His evangelistic zeal began to pay off during the second year when more teachers, mostly at the elementary level, began attending training sessions and student test scores improved for the first time. Within 4 years, the excitement for change and being a part of a new era in the Johnson City schools caught on—with some exceptions at the high school. Champlain was able to breathe life into his vision in 5 short years. A young principal from a poor West Virginia school was so impressed with what he had read about the Johnson City miracle that he loaded 21 of his teachers in a yellow school bus and drove them to Johnson City to learn the mastery teaching and learning model. In 2 years, the success among the students in his West Virginia school was so impressive, he was named state principal of the year. Again, we have one person, one vision, and amazing success.

Visions Are Hard to Realize

The difficulty that leaders face in making a vision happen is twofold. First, many administrators give up on their visions too soon. In a tight job market, most of us like to eat regularly and clothe our families. The overzealous approach by some administrators has produced joblessness. Joan of Arc died for her cause, but educational leaders need to prolong their stay and use good judgment about "when to hold 'em or when to fold 'em." If a community gets into a feeding frenzy about outcome-based education, whole language learning, self-esteem programs, or any other program that causes a major stir, the administrator has to decide whether to be Joan of Arc and attack, or choose to use different language for the programs and live to fight another day. A practical way to keep the vision alive in a time of right-wing and other anti-public school activity is to invite every citizen to contribute to the school visioning process. A word of advice—use the word "vision" with some caution because some people believe that visions appear only to the superreligious or to those who are two pages shy of a book.

One school district that invites contributions is Lewisville, Texas. They seek input from the community on a regular basis by conducting a comprehensive needs assessment every 5 years and annual spot checks to test the community waters. In an effort to involve as wide of a range of groups and individuals as possible, the board and administration decided on a comprehensive, communitywide school needs assessment with a variety of community meetings to invite people to tell the school officials what the patrons wanted the students in Lewisville to know in math, science, language arts, and social studies by the end of the 5th, 8th, and 12th grades. A community survey was designed based on communitywide input and sent to a stratified random sample. Even though the survey instrument was 12 pages long with detailed items, an astonishing 40% returned the surveys for analysis. The receptivity came from the careful planning by the board and administration to include the most vocal critics, senior citizens, students, parents and nonparents, educators, and members of the business and professional communities. The findings of the questionnaire will lead to much greater acceptance by the community—especially the religious right and other vocal adversaries—and the change "pill" will be much easier to swallow. Risk taking is much safer when the homework has been done and the direction of the wind is under constant surveillance. There are times in our administrative lives that a cause is worth losing a job. However, it is good to remember what the old hunting guide said, "Never shoot over the horse's head until the horse is ready."

Remember to learn the ins and outs of any community or organization before you jump up and shoot. Patience, a high boiling point, and a burning vision to build a new and exciting program for your students or clients is an explosive mixture, but leadership is no challenge if the dangers or the excitement are missing in the journey.

Peter Senge (1990), in his book *The Fifth Discipline*, presents one model to help leaders cope with the vicissitudes of change. He believes that the core of any organization is its ability to bring people together to learn new ideas. His "learning organization" concept enables organizations to deal with significant problems facing them and move successfully into the future. Senge believes that the learning organization is primarily designed to help people embrace change. People in learning organizations can look forward to creating, not merely reacting to, the new world as it emerges. It takes time to become an effective learning organization and for team members to develop the skill needed to help them change their work patterns and to interact with others in the organization. This model is the only feasible way to lead people to share a vision.

The content of a shared vision cannot be dictated from on high but must emerge from shared visions. The most powerful motivator is one's own personal vision. The learning organization prizes individual visions and aspirations and builds its future around them. Jack Welch, General Electric's CEO, keeps his learning organization alive by frequent meetings of all employees to create the future. His sessions stress out-of-the-box thinking or, as he says, "boundarylessness" sessions. No rules are established, and all ideas are considered. Perhaps that is why General Electric has grown so dramatically since Welch took over. Risk taking can be reduced if others are involved in the venture. A lone wolf is easy prey when the pack goes in another direction. It is prudent to be safe rather than sorry; remember, change is difficult for all of us unless we thought of the change first or are involved from the very beginning. It is not a sign of weakness to re-vision when your initial vision loses its usefulness or falls on deaf ears. It is your decision about how far and how long you stray from the pack to seek your dream. Father Hesberg, former president of the University of Notre Dame, believes that you must tell your vision to all who will listen with conviction and clarity if you expect acceptance of the ideas in the vision. He said, "You can't blow an uncertain trumpet" (Amundson, 1988, p. 21). If the sound is right and in harmony with those who must make the vision come true, then miracles can happen.

A second difficulty in transforming the vision into reality is the allocation of resources, especially money. If the foundation to the vision is to be built, the money must be there somewhere. If a school has created a collective vision through a democratic process that empowered teachers, students, staff, and parents, the prospects are better for locating external funding through state and federal school improvement assistance programs. Schools that are striving to build learning organizations where collaborative activity is prized and the entire community supports the instructional programs more easily find the resources for enrichment activities for the students. Unless school administrators and the teaching staff create a vision for the school that stresses student learning, team building, and community involvement, funding agencies and corporations are reluctant to add their support. Without new leadership and a new vision for the school or school system, the local and state funding agencies will turn their attention to school leaders who will rally a community for quality and high standards. Funding proposals that stress collaboration, long-range planning, and clear benchmarks for student achievement are generally successful. An example of a principal and teaching staff taking the high road to student achievement is Wesley Elementary School in Houston, Texas. The principal, Thaddeus Lott (personal communication, April 14, 1995), is considered unorthodox by many and a creative leader by others. Lott has become a strong and consistent proponent of basic instruction and strict discipline at a time when it is more popular to talk of outcomes that promote self-esteem and self-paced learning. Thaddeus Lott has fought the school bureaucracy and other educators with his no-nonsense drill and practice instructional programs. Whereas others accused Lott and his teachers of too much drill and of stifling students' creativity, the students continue to learn more than other poor, inner-city kids, and they have high self-esteem.

Lott's success at Wesley convinced the superintendent and the school board to appoint him to manage four schools at once using his winning philosophy. The request to give Lott this expanded role came from a community lay group who wanted all of the elementary children in their area to have the same advantage as the students at Wesley. The school board approved a charter school agreement that will keep the four schools under the Houston school district jurisdiction but will free them of bureaucratic red tape in the key areas of personnel and instruction. This greater autonomy allows Lott to arrange the staff development to create the curriculum and teaching strategies and to seek corporate money to give bonuses to his teachers. Again, we have one person, one vision, and outstanding achievement.

If you, the leader, desire to transform your team vision into reality, then time and reflection are needed to facilitate careful planning and team building. Team building and the use of teams are overlooked areas. Peter Drucker, writing in *The Atlantic Monthly* in November 1994, emphasizes the importance of teams in the knowledge society by indicating that creative individuals in teams will work to improve organizations. New leadership is required to manage these talented, team-oriented organizations toward great productivity. Careful planning involving all stakeholders and continuing to focus on the welfare of the "generic kid" while keeping the overall system in focus will not solve the funding problem, but funding agencies and corporations are steering more grants to schools with a vision of success and empowerment of the entire learning community.

Visionaries Are Rare

Visionaries are in short supply in all organizations. Education and educators are frequently perceived as conservative nonrisk takers who seek the status quo. Exceptions to the conservative security seekers are legion in education, but the perception is still prominent about school personnel. Agriculture and its leadership face the same image problem. Although many agricultural professionals are among the most imaginative and enlightened, others tend to seek conformity and a risk-free role. Duane Ford (1994) writes about a soil scientist, Wes Jackson, who is driven by a vision to create a community based on sustainable agriculture and devoted to stewardship of the earth. Wes Jackson founded the Land Institute in Salina, Kansas, a private research and education organization based on a new model for an agriculture community. The

Land Institute and its adjunct site, Matfield Green, is a village of about 50 people. There, Jackson and the Land Institute have just begun exploring community development on an ecological basis. A perennial polyculture project is aimed at developing the perennial crops needed for such a system. Wild prairie species capable of producing a commercially valuable product are in the process of being domesticated.

The Land Sunshine Farm is a 1-year-old effort projected for a 10-year period. Its aim is to develop and demonstrate a farm run on sunlight and wind rather than fossil fuels. They use a vegetable oil tractor and draft horses, as well as electricity generated with wind and photo voltaic cells. The goal is to see if the farm can be self-sustaining for plant nutrition. Jackson is not taking the attitude of an expert come to save a town; although certainly an ecological missionary, he is not converting people with the sword. He is merely talking and thinking, buying land, rebuilding buildings, starting businesses, and monitoring the village's progress to sustainability. If you go to Matfield Green, stand in front of the old bunkhouse built by the Santa Fe railroad, Wes Jackson's vision will come into focus. In front of you, on the hillsides across the valley, imagine perennial polyculture of grain fields mixed with pastures of the never-plowed prairie so common in the Flint Hills. There is no erosion where prairies or prairie-like crops cover the soil; there is no need for tillage and little need for pesticides or inorganic fertilizers. In the bottom land, imagine a Sunshine Farm producing energy crops and electricity along with conventional crops and livestock. In the distance to the right, imagine Matfield Green, once again the busy hub of a thriving local economy and rich culture. Imagine the whole driven by sunlight and wind. Again, here is one person who is transforming a vision into reality by conserving our natural environment for future generations (Ford, 1994).

Conclusions

Clear, shared visions have a magnetic pull if people are inspired and empowered to help make the vision happen. Individuals can feel alone with their visions unless the leadership encourages the visions to be shared with colleagues. A vision that may be too abstract or "silly" to some may be concrete and serious to others. If the leader(s) can blend individual visions into a school or agency vision, then making the vision happen is possible and creates a symbol of hope for the organization. If the group feels the energy and creative tension in a vision, and the vision is a shared challenge, then the vision can come to pass. Individuals who have a passion for their visions and can persuade others to help make the vision happen are leaders. If a vision is to become a reality, careful planning, time for reflection, and adequate resources are imperative. Impatient managers who run with a vision too fast for those who must make the vision happen will never see a vision fulfilled. A delicate balance between the zeal to make changes and patiently training and empowering others to build strong teams is difficult to manage. The leadership balance and a team plan to seek the resources can help leaders become the visionaries they wish to be. Dreams and visions by leaders can inspire others to extraordinary accomplishments. Leaders for the new millennium must have a dream and share it with others to make it come true.

Techniques to Create "Real-World" Programs

Now that you are "pumped" to create a collective vision and watch the success of your effort pay off in high student or client satisfaction and an excitement for team learning and sharing, what gimmicks or techniques will you use and how will you engage others in the long, difficult journey? What thought process will you adopt to turn your staff into enthusiastic professionals who will give you the respect you deserve? Old Casey Stengel, the famous former New York Yankee manager, knew the value of great team play when he defined leadership as "gettin' paid for home runs somebody else hits" (Amundson, 1988, p. 7). Casey Stengel and other successful leaders realize that they must depend on specialists who can produce the goods. Peter Drucker (1993)believes that the new-knowledge society is moving away from the generalist to the specialist, who must be team oriented. He encourages managers to stress the importance of team workers rather than individuals to stay on the leading edge of the knowledge explosion.

The remainder of this chapter will present futuring strategies to help you and your staff become more visionary and better team players. Stephen Covey (1990) tells us to "begin with the end in mind" (p. 44). This should be used as a frame of reference or, as

Covey refers to it, a personal mission statement. Because personal visions are the most motivating, people need this "inside-out" (p. 62) view to keep them on course. The end in view is not only motivating, it is also fun to share with others. Also, the degree to which each group member feels in control of his or her life and job role will determine the extent to which he or she will contribute to a collaborative effort. A leader who will share power and control and articulate a vision of a high-performing organization will help create the self-esteem and efficacy among staff to help make the vision come true. It is important, then, to invite staff to help plan their own staff development. The following ideas are a good starting point for that important dialogue.

Workshop Activity #1

Divide participants into groups of 8 to 10 persons. Ask the group, "If you could rent the Goodyear blimp and fly it over your community or state in the year 2005, what three professional accomplishments would you flash on the side of the blimp for all to see?" After these personal visions are written down by each individual, ask them to turn to the person at the table located on their right or left and share their visions of their accomplishments. This exercise breaks down barriers between people and gives a feeling of self-esteem and confidence in ideas that most of us do not usually talk about. After both individuals have exchanged their visions, the group facilitator will ask each pair to share their partner's accomplishments with the entire group. Ask the person who had the most recent birthday to be the recorder of each accomplishment on a flip chart for all to see. The facilitator will then ask the group to look for patterns in the accomplishments in 2005 and seek the groups' ideas on what each individual can do to assist the members to accomplish their visions. In all likelihood, several themes will emerge from the desired accomplishments, and the genesis of a collective vision will become obvious. After the group vision takes some shape, rewrite it on the flip chart.

After all groups take a refreshment break, ask the group to appoint a spokesperson to stand and tell the entire workshop crowd the collective group vision and any individual visions that may diverge from the group vision. This step ensures individuality and respect for "out-of-the-box" thinking. Someone should be designated to collect all of the groups' flipcharts and prepare a collective set of staff visions for 2005. These visions can become a driving force in developing a district or system vision. I have used versions of this visioning process with cooperative extension professionals, Phillip Morris executives, church members, school superintendents, principals, and teachers. It is especially effective in districtwide efforts to build a system vision and with site-based teams who need to alter or re-vision based on unforeseen factors that have changed over time.

Workshop Activity #2

This activity works much better in a room with comfortable chairs in a pleasant, quiet atmosphere. Ask the group to begin relaxing and to try to block out the distractions in their busy lives by thinking about personal triumphs in their personal lives. Ask the participants to relax, close their eyes, and imagine themselves 6 years from today on a lakefront or in the mountains in quiet reflection. Ask them to breathe slowly and envision themselves as highly successful, respected professionals in a position where their creativity is prized and their school or organization shares ideas and takes risks to create a superior program with high-quality products and satisfied customers. Ask them what is merely a continuation of past successes and what is new or came from "out of the blue" or from their intuition and has no organizational or personal history? Have them relax even more and lose themselves in creative, new ideas that they wish to share with their colleagues. These ideas should be student or client centered and stress a "cause beyond themselves."

After approximately 5 minutes, ask the group to open their eyes and list the ideas that they envisioned. Following the procedures in the first exercise, ask each participant to turn to the person on the left or right and share the creative thoughts with his or her partner. Ask each group to select a recorder (perhaps the person who owns a cat). Record the individual ideas in round-robin fashion and keep the discussion to a minimum until all ideas are recorded. After all ideas are visible, ask for discussion of any or all items. Next, ask each group to record the most impossible ideas and those that are possible. Ask each group to select two impossible ideas and two possible ideas to share with the entire group. After the entire group has had time to reflect on the most impossible and possible ideas, ask them what must be changed and what obstacles must be overcome to help make any of the impossible ideas become realities. After recording the suggestions, ask them what is necessary to make the possible ideas happen. The discussion usually leads to combining ideas previously considered impossible with those that are viewed as possible (Bishop, 1994). Thus the envelope of the possible is stretched beyond return and a new, exciting idea is born.

This new idea should find a prominent place in the vision statement or mission in the organization. It only takes one idea to ignite an organization to dramatic achievements. Grant Teaff (personal communication, April 14, 1995), former football coach at Baylor University, tells a story about the magic that came from a seemingly impossible idea. Part of his philosophy to build a winning program was to ask his players to write down their personal and team goals at the beginning of the season. In the spring of 1972, a skinny sophomore came in with his written goals and handed them to Teaff. The young athlete then tried to orally repeat the goals, but a speech impediment or stutter made for a prolonged report. Grant Teaff listened as the youngster told him that his goal was to quarterback the Baylor Bears to their first Southwest Conference championship in more than 50 years and lead the team to the Cotton Bowl. After a brief pause while looking into the intense eyes of the young man, Teaff said, "Son, what can I do to help you accomplish your dream?" The coach could have said, "I'm sorry, son, but you and I know that you can't reach your goal as a quarterback with that speech problem." During the quarterback's first season, teammates called the signals in the huddle; in his junior year, he claims that he frequently sang the signals to avoid stuttering. His senior year, Neal Jeffrey clearly called the signals himself and led the Baylor Bears to the first Southwest Conference championship in more than 50

years and to the Cotton Bowl. This 1974 team and its visionary
quarterback became known as the "Miracle on the Brazos." Neal
Jeffrey is now a very successful and articulate minister in Dallas,
Texas.

The impossible to some is possible for others. If the impossible
is to be viewed as possible, the leader must reach beyond the barriers and the obstacles that limit the vision of a staff. Past successes
are frequently the highest barriers to the future. Einstein knew this
well when he said, "No problem can be solved from the same con-
sciousness that created it" (Wheatley, 1992, p. 5). A disgruntled
football fan who was tired of his team losing knew this when he
moaned, "If we keep doin' what we're doin', we're gonna' keep
gettin' what we're gettin'." Margaret Wheatley (1992), author of
Leadership and the New Science, acknowledges that the old ways of
believing that everything is in its place and is predictable and based
on Newtonian physics is under heavy scrutiny by scientists. The
new science, which includes organizational studies, is shifting
from a cause and effect, or top to bottom, precision to unclear relationships that often lack precision and prediction. Wheatley supports the belief that leadership research is changing from power
brokers in charge to individuals in relationships, and from old top-
down bureaucracies to bottom-up empowerment models. In a
speech, she states, "Life always organizes around identity. The first
and greatest need in any project or process is identity, causing us
to ask who we are, why are we choosing to work together, and
what is it that we want to create?" Thus human relationships that
encourage creativity and personal support will help lead to new,
more inclusive organizations where people are free to make things
up as they go along the path to the future. This freedom to create
is the only path to accomplish the impossible. Activity #2 is a good
start toward preparing.

Workshop Activity #3

The following ideas represent a combination of workshop strategies used by Peter Bishop and his colleagues at the Institute for
Futures Research at the University of Houston, Clear Lake cam-

pus, and my own. The purpose of this third exercise is to create a vision for your school or unit, share that vision, and make that vision happen.

Title: Appearing on Global Television to Share a Success Story.

Instructions: Your organization has received word that it has been selected as having one of the three most innovative and client-centered programs in the United States in 2010. The local television affiliate will contact you via interactive TV in 10 minutes to ask you why your organization won the award. What steps were taken early to pave the way for such an honor? What will you say? Ask participants to record their planned remarks for global TV and be prepared to share those with a roving reporter who has arrived in advance to select four participants for the global newscast. The roving reporter, who is the workshop director, moves among the participants and selects several to stand and tell the entire group the secrets to their success as an organization. This step is motivational, often humorous, and focuses on the "end in mind." After the roving reporter completes the interviews, each person who was not interviewed is asked to share with a small group his or her reasons for the award.

Follow this activity by asking each group to investigate what must occur for their school or agency to win such an award by the year 2010. Ask them to think about an organization or company designed to bring about such an award. Next, each group will develop a name for their project, write a brief vision statement, create a logo, and include these things on a flip chart. Find the artist in the group for this task because it will be viewed later by all of the workshop participants. After the group accepts the name of the project or program, vision statement, and logo, the group will write a phrase or motto that describes their vision of the future. Peter Bishop and his colleagues also recommend setting up an art gallery to view all of the group projects and appointing one member of each group to stay with their respective projects to explain it to others.

After all of the artwork has been viewed and explained, begin the process of combining the ideas from each group project. Place all of the projects in front of the combined group and ask each participant to look for similar visions, logos, and mottos. Unless the numbers of participants are too large, this activity creates excellent responses. Ask a colleague to record the comments on flip chart paper and invite one of the better artists to attempt a combined logo. After there is general consensus about the combined effort, ask each group to respond to the following questions: What one thing must change for this vision to become a reality? How will this new direction change how each person does his or her job in the future? What specialized training is necessary for each professional to adjust to the new direction? The combined responses from these questions will prove to be key guides to designing the goal statements, activities, and evaluation strategies. This step empowers the school faculty to take a realistic look at their future and to visualize and hold in their mind's eye a school where all faculty and students perform at high levels, have respect for each other, and contribute to each other's welfare.

Workshop Activity #4

This exercise, Schools for the Future, helps a faculty envision a school that provides total human service for all students.

Activity: Future school and student project. Divide staff into five- to six-member multigrade and subject-area faculty.

Resources: Selected articles from *The Futurist*, a journal which is published six times annually by the World Future Society, 4916 St. Elmo Ave., Bethesda, MD 20814.

The School of the Future by P. Schlecty, published by Jossey-Bass.

School Empowerment, edited by M. Richardson, M. Flanagan, and K. Lane, published by Technomic Publishing Co. See Chapter 10, "A Vision of the Future and the New School Principal," by J. Hoyle.

Flip chart pad with easels and felt tip pens for each group.

Session1: School for the Future—Part 1.

Task: Create a school of the future that includes complete human services for all students (i.e., health care, family services, etc.). Each group will begin by listing the kinds of skills, attributes, knowledge, and values that the faculty would like the students to have when they graduate from their school. The second step is to create the most appropriate learning experiences for teaching those desired attributes.

Time: 2½ hours.

Session 2: School for the Future—Part 2.

Task: Each group will render a drawing of their school on the flip chart pad. The drawing will include the shape and size of the facility, the learning areas, and external features (i.e., recreation, community agencies, etc.).

Time: 2 hours.

This Schools for the Future exercise can be expanded to a communitywide activity to include significant stakeholders in the school, especially representatives from the other human service agencies and the business and religious representatives. Expanded to other stakeholders or not, this exercise has several implications for building shared visions on school planning. Each faculty group will discuss the implications of the shared school vision on current curriculum, teaching, testing, technology, and school organization. Also, the entire faculty will come together to discuss the next steps necessary to build the future school that will produce students with the necessary attributes to make them successful in the 21st century. The extent to which the shared vision of the future school becomes a reality rests with the enthusiastic support of the superintendent, school board, and the school principal. The faculty will stay focused on the vision only if the leadership is there to constantly encourage them. These suggested staff development sessions will help create a spark of creativity, promote a sharing of newer ideas among the entire staff, and improve classroom teaching and student performance.

Workshop Activity #5

Scenario writing was made popular by the late Herman Kahn, author of books such as *On ThermoNuclear War*, *The Coming Boom*, and *The Next 200 Years*. Kahn directed the Hudson Institute and was a leading advisor and consultant for the Office of the President, the Department of Defense, and major corporations. His most effective futures methodology was the scenario. He would study historical and current trends, global economics, politics, and new technologies before embarking on preparing three scenarios based on assumptions and three sets of data. This approach would offer Kahn's clients alternative futures (i.e., preferred, acceptable, unacceptable). He believed that we can choose which alternative we prefer and can have some influence on which alternative happens.

Creating Scenarios

A scenario is developed by studying all possible information about a problem and projecting a broad range of trends, their likelihood of occurrence, and the degree of impact on the organization under study if the trends did occur. In writing scenarios, imagine your life at some future time—such as 10, 15, or 20 years from now. Describe your future as if you are there now! The scenario in Chapter 2 written by the high school junior is an example of leaping into the future and describing your job role, the world around you, your family, transportation, education system and learning technologies, community development, and so on. Describe how you feel about your new world and what you have accomplished. Include the education and professional development that helped promote you to your exalted position in, say, 2008. Scenario writing should follow immediately after earlier exercises that stressed imaging and futuring. The length of a scenario can range from one paragraph to several pages. The length for the following exercise is recommended to be no more than one page. This length will allow time for participants to share their masterpieces with each other. This sharing is fun, exciting, and encourages creative "out-of-the-box" thinking. Scenarios contain the following benefits:

1. They make us aware of potential pitfalls that may occur if a certain action is taken. Scenarios make it possible to consider the possible circumstances of a proposed action and assist us in altering the action to avoid negative consequences (Bishop, 1994).
2. Scenarios give us an opportunity to think about our future successes as individuals and as organizations.
3. All age groups, especially students, enjoy writing scenarios because they are not typical term research papers or reports. Elementary school teachers already know this. I have read scenarios by fourth graders that are research based, creative, and well organized.

4. Scenarios can rally others to work in teams to analyze alternative plans and actively participate in building programs.

5. Scenarios spark imagination, create emotion, and bring about an awareness of broad trends and issues; scenarios are easy to read and they enable the individual to see how he or she fits into the scheme of things. Remember, personal visions are the most powerful.

Scenario Exercise

This exercise should follow Workshop Activity #2, which included the relaxation and visioning process, or Workshop Activity #4, the Schools for the Future activity. The data and ideas generated by the group members will prepare them for writing the scenario. Allow 10 to 15 minutes for writing, and follow with the roving reporter and invite volunteers to share their future with the entire group. In a recent workshop for young political hopefuls in Austin, Texas, I found an enthusiastic young African American woman who read about her future as governor in 20 years. Scenarios have a strong future pull about them, so who am I to question her election? Asking people to share their future creates good humor and deep reflection on preferred futures for all participants. Last year, a graduate student named Debbie, a talented musician, told her scenario to the class while playing a piano. She said, "I will own and manage my own school, which will stress music therapy, and will meet the love of my life named David." Recently, I ran into Debbie at the mall and she ran up, hugged me, and exclaimed, "You are not going to believe this, but I recently got a job as a music therapist and I am engaged to be married in June. His name is David!" A coincidence? No one can predict the future, but scenarios can lead one's thinking in interesting directions.

Organizations, including schools, universities, cooperative extension programs, and other human service agencies, can move beyond the ordinary strategic planning processes that are often boring and viewed by the staff as something done by a consultant or committee. Staff interest in team planning can be raised to new, higher levels by conducting the exercises in this chapter and culminating with a series of scenarios to be examined by all stakeholders for possible action. In my 38 years in education, scenario writing is the most effective method I have found to motivate students and professionals to think seriously about their future and how the world will affect that future.

Tech Prep: A Scenario for 2015

The following scenario is part of a keynote address I gave. This vision of Tech Prep and its future possibilities is an example of how a scenario can be an excellent motivational device to focus a group on their own vision. I asked the audience to imagine reading an article from the *Houston Chronicle* on February 10, 2015.

Tech prep programs were given high praise by the keynote speaker at the 22nd annual Gulf Coast Consortium Spring Tech Prep Conference. Dr. David Sanders, President of Power Infotech Systems, said, "I am impressed. This tech prep program serves over 3 million people in the Gulf Coast area and is a model integrating the education resources of public schools, higher education, government, business, and social service agencies into serving the needs of people. Education is really working." The 22nd conference was held in the new Tech Prep Center, which is a futuristic masterpiece. The center houses specialists in information technologies, urban planners, education and health specialists, and business and family counselors. These specialists facilitate the learning and development of students, teachers, and community members with new job skills and self-esteem. Equipped with the big four information technologies—computer networks, imaging technology, massive data storage, and artificial intelligence—the center and its staff are helping Gulf Coast citizens learn to use them more skillfully and effectively. Dr. Sanders told the audience that national information highways allow tech prep students and clients to communicate with anyone, anywhere, anytime. Through imaging technologies, students from preschool through graduate school can actually learn by doing. New job skills are mastered through virtual reality and other visual models. Equipped with color video phones connected to schools, homes, businesses, and learning centers, clients can send and receive digital visual information from center specialist to classrooms, corporate boardrooms, businesses, and homes. Throughout the Gulf Coast region, students can beam up the Tech Prep Center and get help with math, languages, sciences, job skills, and personal counseling on financial or psychological problems. These interactive learning technologies have been a prime factor in the high achievement of students in the K-12 and community college systems.

The quality of the workforce is considered the best in the South and Southwest. These remarkable achievements had their genesis in the 1980s and grew dramatically in the 1990s. In 1994, at the first annual Gulf Coast conference, several visionaries gathered to create a successful future for tech prep. These leaders knew that the old image of vocational education was a barrier to the new image of tech prep. The old vocational programs, which were dropping in enrollment, were considered by some as "not very demanding," and Carl Perkins funding for the faltering programs was in jeopardy. Through a process of re-visioning a new tech prep model of success, a dream was begun. Integrating academic, career, and technology content with staff development to train teacher and workforce groups, a new integrated curriculum was initiated. This new contextual model changed the perception of career and technology education into meaning-centered education. Students were exposed to future career opportunities and experienced the reasons that math, English, languages, and science are critical to success in the labor force. By mediated learning technologies, job site visits, and mentors, students and teachers at all levels viewed career and academic learning as one program. It was education with meaning and quality.

Gulf Coast middle school, high school, and community college students are 25 minutes from the Tech Prep Center via mag-lev high-speed rail. At the center, students can access classes at community colleges, high schools, universities, and corporations via interactive compressed video. Dr. Sanders also stated that "the Gulf Coast area is among the top five most productive urban centers in America. We have 2% unemployment, fourth highest per capita income, and violence and crime rates are reduced over 70% since 1994." Many reasons are given for this phenomenal reversal, but observers pointed to the tech prep program leaders, who persuaded traditional educators, business, and government leaders that every child, college bound or not, needs self-esteem and meaning. Tech prep educators knew that the jobs of the future were in the medical, business, engineering, and legal services; careers in air transportation and information, recreation, and health were also among the bright careers. From 1989 to 1994, Texas led the nation in job growth and had the highest percentage of young people for the future workforce. This diverse multilingual future workforce needed skills and self-esteem to become productive members of society who could have a quality life in safe and caring communities. Education and job skills were the answer to a successful 21st century in the Gulf Coast area.

Back in the winter of 1994, the future was cloudy and frightening for those gathered at that first Tech Prep conference. Regular public education programs were educating about 40% of the students. The others were sent into an information-based job market with minimum skills and little promise of success in life. Add this to the high poverty rate, especially among minority youth from single-parent homes in the Gulf Coast region, and there existed a pattern of violence, fear, and day-to-day survival that was thrown to the schools to handle. The American dream for many of our kids in 1994 had become a nightmare of despair.

The education models in 1994 were not working, and tech prep leaders heeded the words of Margaret J. Wheatley, author of a 1992 book titled *Leadership and the New Science,* who believes that we create reality as we go along, not because we are not good planners, but because reality is difficult to find and the search can bring meaning to our lives and work.

With a vision for collaboration and a growing comfort with uncertainty, tech prep consortium members moved beyond the dream. These ideas might have languished, but fortunately, new Carl Perkins funds, state appropriations, client fees, and corporate and local funding made the dream a reality. The Tech Prep Center was completed 6 years ago, in 2009. Only a small number of those attending that first conference in February of 1994 believed that the facility would become a reality and that tech prep would dramatically give direction to education and the Gulf Coast area. The dream came true. [End of article]

Conclusions

To become the leader who can persuade your staff to engage in futuring, you need to practice your futuring skills. Darrell Royal, who coached the University of Texas Longhorns to national championships and many bowl victories, believed that how a team practices was the difference between the winners and losers. He said, "If my life depended on chopping down a big tree in one hour, I would spend the first 30 minutes sharpening my ax." Practice your skills of persuasion and visioning on a daily basis. Begin with a small steering committee and train them to train others in futuring using the exercises in this chapter, or arrange for you and the committee to attend futuring sessions offered by individuals or professional associations. Futuring encompasses the major components of other development activities, such as total quality management, quality circles, strategic planning, and team building processes. Futuring conveys images of the future, captures the assumptions and forces affecting the future, and creates an excitement for team play. Max De Pree (1989), author of *Leadership Is an Art*, said it all about the importance of a leader keeping the ax of leadership sharp when he wrote, "In the end, it is important to remember that we cannot become what we need to be by remaining what we are" (p. 100).

The Visionary Leader
You Can Become

Pat Riley (1993), philosopher and coach of the New York Knicks, knows the dangers of resting on last year's performance and warns us by saying, "Excellence is the gradual result of always wanting to do better." This book is about how to get better as visionary leaders for schools and other organizations.

All school administrators and educators I know want to get better at what they do. However, those I know who are constantly talking about the future are the ones who seem to get more done and with more flair. These individuals spend their time learning new ideas by talking to others and participating in workshops about change and how to bring it about. They realize that skills in futuring and visioning are critical to their success and to how they feel about themselves as leaders. Max De Pree (1989) understood this when he said, "The only kind of leadership worth following is based on vision" (p. 133). Many leading school superintendents said they like to think about the future and build a vision of what is best for kids, but they do not like to wait too long to make a decision. If they do, the school board and the staff think the superintendent is indecisive or burned out. School leaders tend to get bored without a challenge and would prefer to be viewed as a "mover and shaker" rather than a visionary and dreamer. Most visionaries are impatient about the status quo because their visions haunt them. Thus they face the dilemma of vision building and bringing others along to create ownership, and the impatience to make things happen now. Richard Wallace, former superintendent of the Pittsburgh schools, is a dynamic leader who is both impatient and team oriented. He advises others to "articulate to various constituencies your vision of the educational process and better outcomes" (Lewis, 1993, p. 8). According to one of Wallace's colleagues, Wallace was a tough decision maker. "If he was not sure about the right decision he would gather all of the information he could in the time he had, but as soon as his mind was made up he trusted his own instincts and it was very difficult to change after that" (Lewis, 1993, p. 9). Social scientists have few clues about the makeup of charismatic visionary leaders like Richard Wallace. Jay Conger (1989), in his book *The Charismatic Leader,* presents his view of the characteristics of charismatic visionaries. He writes,

Charismatic leaders were great information collectors with a difference—they used multiple and often apparently unrelated sources of information. . . . The second element of vision involves risk. Launching a new product or service . . . sometimes involves extreme risk. . . . Timing and serendipity are also critical elements in whether the strategic vision will ultimately materialize into success. (pp. 66, 67)

Conger and others have found that subordinates of visionaries tend to like their jobs more, work longer hours without complaint, trust colleagues and their leaders more, and have higher performance ratings than the followers of nonvisionary leaders (Conger, 1989). Visionary leaders seem to develop team loyalty around ideas and shared values. Also, visionaries can be iconoclasts by going against the grain, but they can also inspire staff to cultivate the organizational culture by using metaphors, shared symbols, mottos, and a sense of history and purpose to cause others to rally to a cause.

The six leaders I described in Chapter 1 were blessed with charisma and vision. The leaders I knew and those I didn't had that undefined ability to move ordinary people to extraordinary accomplishments. That is why I remember them and why history recorded them. They had a capacity for caring for others, clear communication, and a commitment to persist. These characteristics, then, are the legs on which to stand if you wish to improve your vision and be seen as a more charismatic leader.

Leaders Care About Others

The capacity to care deeply is embedded in one's moral center and core values. How you acquire it is generally known in social science research. Childhood and all of its influences are considered the foundation for becoming a caring visionary leader. Psychologist David McClelland (1978) has spent a career investigating the characteristics of high achievers. He found that high achievers tend to have four basic behavioral characteristics: (a) the willingness to take moderate, calculated risks; (b) a preference for activities that provide rapid and precise information on the nature of the problems as well as performance; (c) intrinsic satisfaction in getting a job done well rather than extrinsic rewards; and (d) a preoccupation with completing a task, often at the expense of interpersonal relationships. Thus a high need to achieve can get in the way of getting along and caring about others in the organization. The visionary leader for the future must be impatient to make visions happen, but only to the extent that others in the organization know that the leader is sensitive to their needs and will take the time to inform and train them for the challenge ahead. A visionary is not very valuable unless he or she can bring others along to help build the vision.

Caring for others is the motivator for most of us who chose education as a career and for others who entered the ministry, youth work, or social welfare agencies. Albert Schweitzer gave up a prominent and lucrative medical practice to spend his life healing the sick in the jungles of Africa. Mother Teresa, a symbol of love for those destitute in India, could have chosen a less demanding and more comfortable life. Those of us who chose to educate others may not spend our lives among the sick and helpless, but our challenge to become servant leaders is equally important. Each time we explain our vision and attempt to persuade others to help us blaze a new path, we are asking them to believe in us and to go along with the risks in the unknown. Futurist Joel Barker knows the value and the risks in developing a collective vision in any organization. The leader is ultimately responsible for the final product. It is this vision, belief, and trust in others that can make a vision happen. Barker, in his video titled *The Power of Vision*, says, "Vision without action goes nowhere, vision with action can change the world." Compassion for the well-being of others can produce the necessary action to make a dream become a reality. Camille Lavington, an international image and marketing consultant believes that by serving others selflessly and helping them achieve their highest goals, everyone will benefit from their abilities and achievements. Visionary leaders must have a cause beyond a personal agenda or self-enhancement.

What, then, can you do to become a more caring person and leader? People will follow servant leaders who model the team concept. Arlene Blum led nine other women to accomplish something that no other group of women had done. She led the American Women's Himalayan Expedition to reach the summit of Annapurna 1, the 10th highest mountain in the world. She spoke the words of a true servant leader when she said of their accomplishment,

> We had to believe in ourselves enough to make the attempt in spite of social convention and two hundred years of climbing history in which women had been told that they didn't have the leadership experience and emotional stability necessary to climb the highest mountains. (Kouzes & Posner, 1987, p. 82)

A servant leader who persuaded nine other women to take a major risk, Arlene Blum told of her vision, helped the other women gain the necessary skills and confidence to accept the challenge, and the mountain became theirs.

Because school reform has begun to change the face of education, a new, more caring leader is required to facilitate the changes. With greater emphasis on empowering others and fostering greater creativity and risk taking, principals and teachers must share the leadership functions. This systemic change to more bottom-up leadership is frequently viewed as a challenge to the power and autonomy of school boards and central office administrators and can create roadblocks to visions for faculty, students, and parents. However, the caring superintendent will shift the focus of power and authority to others to encourage the visioning process to flourish. Remember—when you become obsessed with your own importance, visions grow dim and the ability to motivate others dies. Unless the leader is viewed as a caring, serving person, others try to avoid him or her. Robert K. Greenleaf (1991), in his book *Servant Leadership*, tells us that people will follow leaders who serve them first and then lead them to higher, exciting goals through clear vision and encouragement. To become more caring is not something that you wake up on Monday and decide to do. You must practice the habits of caring and kindness over and over until the habit has you. Caring, compassionate leaders seem to love life a little more than do others. They have a good sense of humor and can bring smiles that chase away the hurt and failure in others' lives. Caring leaders, according to Max De Pree (1989), "don't inflict pain, they bear pain" (p. 11).

Leaders who have developed a capacity for caring hold power over others. A power of admiration and respect and an image of well-being, strength, and energy seem to shine in those who care for others and their welfare. Mehrabian (1971), a behavioral scientist, found that leaders affect the perceptions of others threefold. Visual impact is 55%, vocal impact is 38%, and the words you use have an impact of only 7%. Obviously, this researcher found that the way you look and sound in trying to influence others to buy into your vision is far more important than the words you use. Social psychologists tell us that first impressions are the most lasting, which adds validity to the visual impact of 55%. However, communications specialists warn of trying to separate the message from the messenger. The bearer of the vision will have far greater success if he or she is viewed as a caring, compassionate person. The way you appear to others has an obvious impact on your ability to lead them to make a vision a reality. If you can clearly articulate the story and concentrate on the why of the vision rather than the how, you will be successful. Victor Frankl (1967), author of *Man's Search for Meaning*, spent 3 years as a prisoner in Auschwitz and remained alive under horrible conditions because he knew the "why" of life. He believed that if something in the future was expected (i.e., seeing your child again or finishing a rare manuscript or project), you could stay alive. He wrote,

> A man who becomes conscious of the responsibility he bears toward a human being who affectionately waits for him, or an unfinished work, will never be able to throw away his life. He knows the "why" for his existence and will be able to bear almost any "how." (p. 127)

A compassionate caring for others is the essence of life and leadership.

Leaders Communicate Clearly

Next, visionary leaders are master communicators, often not for what they say but what they do. Mrs. Shunantona did not tell me how to learn more math the morning I came to her class feeling like a complete failure. She skipped the math sermon and told the class that I was the best first baseman she had ever seen. But I did become a better math student. Dr. Hensarling did not give me a lecture on "quitters never win" or plead with me to stay in the doctoral program to ensure my future. No, he said, "Be better than you think you can be." I took the message to heart and completed my doctorate. Paul Salmon did not tell me that the preparation guidelines were acceptable; he said, "Where are the kids in these guidelines?" The words and the meanings were clear, and they came at a time when I needed to hear them. These leaders knew that "to communicate effectively, the sender's words and symbols must mean the same thing to the receiver that they do to the sender" (Cutlip, Center, & Broom, 1985, p. 261). It takes more than facts to persuade others. Actions sometimes do speak louder than words, and most people would rather see a good example than hear one.

   Our word choice and use are also keys to persuading others. A story out of World War II illustrates the value of clear, carefully chosen words to persuade.

   Col. David Shoup served as a Marine commander in the battle for Tarawa in the South Pacific. Tarawa, said the Japanese, would never be taken by a million men in 100 years because of the bunkers, pill boxes, and bomb-proof blockhouses. During an intense firefight to take an airstrip, a young officer ran into Col. Shoup's command post crying that his men couldn't advance because of a machine gun. Disgusted, Shoup responded that it was only one machine gun. The young officer ran back to his men under a hail of gunfire. In a few minutes, he returned to Shoup's command post complaining that there were a thousand marines dug in on the beach and that not one of them would follow him across the air strip to attack the Japanese. Shoup told him that he had to ask who would follow him. He advised that if the officer could get only 10 men to follow him, that 10 was better than none. The young officer clearly got the message and returned for good this time. He led his men to victory and turned the tide of the battle for Tarawa. Clear words filled with emotion and purpose under the most difficult of circumstances moved a thousand Marines to win a major battle. Colonel David Shoup later became General Shoup, Commander of the U.S. Marine Corps. His effective skills in communication helped others see the vision of victory (Leckie, 1978).

   School leaders can improve their visionary skills by developing a stronger vocabulary and becoming more selective of the words they use. The right words will help rally teachers, parents, and community members in establishing local goals and procedures to improve teaching and learning for all students. The skill of clearly communicating student achievement data and the best strategies to align good teaching with good testing is a an example of visionary leadership. Richard Wallace advises other school leaders that "they must envision strengthened schools and be able to energize professionals and the community to bring about the conditions that will ensure a high-quality educational product" (Lewis, 1993, p. 8). This "energizing" occurs through the message the leader brings to the people.

A final but equally important communication skill is the art of listening. When you ignore someone talking to you, it is the height of arrogance. It tells the other person that you consider yourself to be superior to him or her. A former sociology professor of mine, Dr. Dan Davis, better known as "Cigar Dan" because of the stub of a cigar permanently positioned in the corner of his mouth, told this story in a lecture about listening to others. He said,

> I have seen the horrors of the Nazi concentration camps. Later I worked in Pakistan and witnessed children literally starve to death. But let me tell you something, class, the cruelest form of punishment that one person can inflict upon another is lack of recognition of their existence. If you want to destroy a relationship with another person or close them out of your life forever, stop listening to them.

Good listeners are good communicators. Practice listening to those you love and care about the most, your family, and see if communication improves in your household. Next, practice the listening skills on the job and see the immediate effect on creating shared visions.

Leaders Don't Give Up

Visionary leaders always finish the race they begin. This commitment to persist separates the wild blue skiers from the high flyers in learning organizations. Good lead-off hitters are vital to baseball teams, but without the clean-up hitters to drive in the runs, they can't win. Organizations need leaders who can get on base to start the rally and then drive in the runs. Inert ideas abound in all institutions because no individual or group will follow up to drive the idea home. Winston Churchill never started a race he didn't finish. Disappointments and failures never quenched his fire of persistence. Three-time Olympic gold medalist Wilma Rudolph never quit anything she started until death took her at age 54. According to an Associated Press release by Teresa M. Walker, Wilma's race in life got off to a rough start. The 20th of 22 children, Rudolph fought through double pneumonia at age 4 and scarlet fever that had her parents thinking she would die. Later, she was stricken with polio, which doctors thought would keep her from walking. With the love and help of her family, who massaged her withered legs, and a cumbersome brace on her left leg, she learned to walk. At age 9, she was required to wear an unattractive high-top shoe. Her burning desire to recover led to the track, where she later inspired the world in the 1960 Olympics in Rome by winning gold medals in the 100- and 200-meter races and the 400-meter relay. Wilma did not rest on her laurels; she became a successful teacher, businesswoman, coach, lecturer, and president of the Wilma Rudolph Foundation, which was dedicated to teaching youngsters to overcome obstacles in their lives. After she won the gold medals, the city of Clarksville, Tennessee, wanted to have a victory celebration for her homecoming. Because her town was segregated at the time, Wilma Rudolph refused to participate in a victory parade unless it was integrated for everyone. With this gesture of love, she brought her hometown together as one people. She was a sharing, caring person who had vision for her race and for children who needed a boost in life. Tennessee governor Ned McWorter eulogized her this way: "Wilma Rudolph's greatest race was not on the field. Her greatest race was won through her experiences throughout her life. The race included many hurdles. She overcame them to become one of the most famous athletes in history." Wilma Rudolph started and finished the race. Her qualities of persistence are models for all of us who attempt to lead others to a better future.

School leaders faced with critical publics, budget cuts, rules, and policies to regulate everything from asbestos to Xerox need all of the Rudolph grit they can muster. New developments in learning technologies and the knowledge society place school principals between superintendents who want better test scores and more National Merit Finalists and parents who demand special programs for "their children." Teachers invariably complain about parents, not about the students. Recently, a young first-grade teacher told me, "If it were not for the irrational parents, my job would be wonderful." Parents are worried about the future and how their children will survive without the best education, and they turn their anxiety toward the educators, who perceive it to be criticism. Peter Drucker (1993), in his book *Post-Capitalist Society*, heightens the pressures on educators by reminding us that education is the center of the knowledge society and challenges educators to help learners center on the most important knowledge and new ways to teach that knowledge. Faced with these and other daunting questions, it is easier to abandon ship and leave the challenges to future generations of educators. Dr. Paul Hensarling's words keep returning to all of his former students who want to drop out of the race. "Be better than you think you can be" strikes at the heart of a true professional who has a vision for better schools and a better society for all people. Many of the most talented and visionary school leaders I know are tired of the hassles that come with public service in education. They, along with cooperative extension and other human service agency leaders, are taking early retirement. Although this break from high visibility and pressure is understandable and well earned, I weep for the communities and children who will lose a person at the young age of 55 or 60 with accumulated knowledge that can never be replaced. In fact, recent research by Lydia Bronte (1993) found that more than half of the 150 Americans she interviewed who made significant achievements started their period of peak creativity after age 50. Bronte contends that because people are living longer and have better health at older ages, we have expanded the meaning of middle age. She believes that the new middle age is 50 to 75 years. They are healthy and energetic, but they seem to have lost their spark for life or the challenge in their jobs. I ask my middle-aged friends if they have finished the race. My question may be unfair, but it is asked with the best of intentions to persuade a mature leader to reconsider leaving the race so early. He or she has spent a lifetime learning, gaining respect from a wide constituency, and making immeasurable contributions to the community, state, and nation. How about you, the reader of this short book on visionary leadership? Will your vision go unfinished? Will the ideas you have tried to implement fall on fallow soil because you were not there to cultivate them and make them grow into a reality for kids or clients? Finish the race and make your vision become a reality.

Conclusions

To become the kind of person and visionary leader you wish to be is obviously more complex than following the instructions included in this chapter. Stephen Covey (1990), in his *Principle-Centered Leadership*, realizes that there are many problems that occur in our daily lives that are difficult to solve using good common practices. Natural laws of the universe are at work that pertain to human relationships and human organizations. To violate these natural laws can lead to disappointment and failure in our leadership roles. Covey believes that leaders of men and women should build these natural laws into the center of their lives and into their management practices. Principle-centered leadership is practiced from the inside out on four levels: (a) personal, which is one's relationship with others; (b) interpersonal, which is one's relationship and interactions with others; (c) managerial, which is one's responsibility to get the job done with others; and (d) organizational, which is one's need to organize people, to recruit them, train them, and compensate them; to build teams; to solve problems; and to create aligned structures, strategies, and systems (Covey, 1990, p. 3).

Covey and others who write about the leadership and vision connection reinforce the three characteristics of the leaders I knew or wish I had known: a capacity for caring for others, communication with clear and visionary ideas, and a commitment to persist. These three characteristics encompass Covey's natural laws of human interaction; that is, relationships and interactions with others, working with others to get the job done, and helping others gain the skills and confidence to pursue a vision of success are the skills that were basic to the leadership of Mrs. Shunantona, Dr. Hensarling, Dr. Salmon, Jesus of Nazareth, Joan of Arc, and Winston Churchill. Work on improving your skill in these three areas, and watch your servant leadership skills improve and your influence expand. Visionary leaders can be developed, and the ability to persuade others to join you in the pursuit of your dream can happen. It is up to you.

Annotated Bibliography
and References

Annotated Bibliography

Barna, G. (1990). *The frog in the kettle.* Ventura, CA: Regal.

An excellent account of changing societal issues of religion, family, and demographic distributions. Barna presents compelling reasons to plan for the future rather than suffering the consequences of only reacting to change.

Bolman, L., & Deal, T. (1993). *The path to school leadership.* Newbury Park, CA: Corwin.

A well-written, practical look at "real-world" leadership through the use of dialogue between administrators and staff.

Chance, E. (1992). *Visionary leadership in schools.* Springfield, IL: Charles C Thomas.

Chance presents strategies to assist school leaders in developing shared visions for school improvement. He lists several helpful workshop activities for facilitating the visioning process.

Conger, J. (1989). *The charismatic leader.* San Francisco: Jossey-Bass.

A very interesting look at charismatic, visionary leaders and the processes they use to empower others to share visions.

Chapter 9, "Developing Exceptional Leadership in Organizations," includes suggestions about visioning skills, trust-building skills, and empowerment skills. The research base adds credibility to this excellent book.

Covey, S. (1990). *Principle-centered leadership.* New York: Simon & Schuster.

Covey incorporates the seven habits of highly effective people into this classic work. Principle-centered leaders are men and women of character who work with competence on the basis of natural principles and who build those principles into the center of their lives. The center is the moral compass to guide the leader to empower others.

Drucker, P. (1993). *Post-capitalist society.* New York: Harper.

An exceptional description of social transformations in the 20th century with special emphasis on knowledge workers, who will give the emerging knowledge society its character and its leadership. He proclaims that education will become the center for the knowledge society and that specialized knowledge will be the key to visionary leadership.

Hoyle, J., English, F., & Steffy, B. (1994). *Skills for successful school leaders* (2nd ed., rev.). Arlington, VA: American Association of School Administrators.

This popular text presents nine knowledge/skill areas that provide the foundation for the field of educational administration. Each chapter includes a self-help checklist to assist the university professor and student in improving their visionary leadership.

Kennedy, P. (1993). *Preparing for the 21st century.* New York: Random House.

A comprehensive look at the global population projections, technological advances, food and fiber production and distribution, communications, conflict, and community development. An excellent study of the 21st century.

Kouzes, J., & Posner, B. (1987). *The leadership challenge.* San Francisco: Jossey-Bass.

The book begins with a clear, practical description of leaders at their best and provides five practices and 10 commandments. Part 3 is especially relevant to help the reader gain skills in inspiring a shared vision and how to attract people to common purposes.

Russell, C. (1993). *The master trend: How the baby boom generation is making America.* New York: Plenum.
A look at the impact of baby boomers and their offspring on the future of America. Issues of education, the labor market, families, health care, and retirement are presented to challenge the thinking of leaders in education and other human service agencies.

References

Amundson, K. (1988). *Challenges for school leaders.* Arlington, VA: American Association of School Administrators.

Banfield, S. (1985). *Joan of Arc.* New York: Chelsea House.

Bishop, P. (1994, December). Project 2020 Vision Workshop directory and lecture notes. Dallas, TX.

Bronte, L. (1993). *The longevity factor.* New York: HarperCollins.

Brooks, P. (1956). The greatest life ever lived. In W. B. Gamble, *Well said: Benedicte's scrapbook.* Grand Rapids, MI: W. B. Eerdmans.

Conger, J. (1989). *The charismatic leader.* San Francisco: Jossey-Bass.

Covey, S. R. (1990). *Principle-centered leadership.* New York: Simon & Schuster.

Cutlip, S. M., Center, A. H., & Broom, G. M. (1985). *Effective public relations* (6th ed.). Englewood Cliffs, NJ: Prentice-Hall.

De Pree, M. (1989). *Leadership is an art.* New York: Dell.

Drucker, P. (1993). *Post-capitalist society.* New York: Harper Business.

Drucker, P. (1994). The age of social transformation. *The Atlantic Monthly,* November, 53-80.

Ford, D. (1994, July/August). *The land sunshine farm* [Newsletter]. College Station, TX: Texas A&M University, Center for Biotechnology Policy and Ethics.

Frankl, V. (1967). *Man's search for meaning.* New York: Washington Square.

Greenleaf, R. K. (1991). *Servant leadership: A journey into the nature of legitimate power and greatness.* Mohwah, NJ: Paulist.

Hoyle, J., English, F., & Steffy, B. (1985). *Skills for successful school leaders.* Arlington, VA: American Association of School Administrators.

Kennedy, P. (1993). *Preparing for the 21st century.* New York: Random House.

Kouzes, J., & Posner, B. (1987). *The leadership challenge.* San Francisco: Jossey-Bass.

Leckie, R. (1978). Tarawa: Conquest of the unconquerable. In *Readers Digest illustrated stories of World War II* (pp. 236-249). Pleasantville, NY: Readers Digest Association.

Lewis, A. (1993). *Leadership styles.* Arlington, VA: American Association of School Administrators.

Manchester, W. (1983). *The last lion: Winston Spencer Churchill: Visions of glory, 1874-1932.* Boston: Little, Brown.

Manners, G. E., & Steger, J. A. (1979). The implications of research on the R&D manager's role to the selection and training of scientists and engineers for management. *R&D Management, 9,* 85-92.

McClelland, D. (1978). The two faces of power. In D. Hampton, C. Sumner, & R. Webber (Eds.), *Organizational behavior and practices of management* (p. 30). Glenview, IL: Scott, Foresman.

Mehrabian, A. (1971). *Silent messages.* Belmont, CA: Wadsworth.

Riley, P. (1993). *The winner within.* New York: G. P. Putnam & Son.

Rogers, J. (1986). *Winston Churchill.* New York: Chelsea House.

Rowan, R. (1986). *The intuitive manager.* New York: Berkeley Books.

Scruggs, J. C., & Swerdlow, J. L. (1985). *To heal a nation.* New York: Harper & Row.

Senge, P. (1990). *The fifth discipline.* New York: Doubleday.

Wheatley, M. (1992). *Leadership and the new science.* San Francisco: Berrett-Koehler.